how to Raise Your Parents

A Teen Girl's Survival Guide

how to **Raise Your Parents**
A Teen Girl's Survival Guide

By Sarah O'Leary Burningham
Illustrations by Bella Pilar

chronicle books · san francisco

Dave,
age 17

Julie,
age 17

For my parents
—Sarah O'Leary Burningham

For my daughter, who will one day read and love it!
—Bella Pilar

Note: To protect teenagers who shared their stories,
some names have been changed.

Text © 2008 by Sarah O'Leary Burningham.
Illustrations © 2008 by Bella Pilar.

Book design by Mariana Oldenburg.
Typeset in Futura.
The illustrations in this book were rendered in gouache paint.
Manufactured in China.

Library of Congress Cataloging-in-Publication Data
Burningham, Sarah O'Leary.
How to raise your parents : a teen girl's survival guide / by Sarah O'Leary Burningham ; illustrated by Bella Pilar.
    p. cm.
ISBN 978-0-8118-5696-6
1. Parent and teenager. 2. Teenage girls—United States—Attitudes. 3. Teenage girls—Conduct of life. 4.
Teenage girls—Life skills guides. 5. Communication in the family. I. Title.
HQ799.15.B86 2008
646.7'80835—dc22
2007010034

10 9 8 7 6 5 4 3 2 1

Chronicle Books LLC
680 Second Street, San Francisco, California 94107

www.chroniclekids.com

Contents

Introduction

Parents Should Come with Instruction Booklets

Five Reasons It Rocks to Be a Teenager

1. You're not a kid anymore
2. You don't have to pay taxes
3. Summer vacation
4. Prom night and that super-hot dress you're going to wear
5. When you're in a bad mood, you can blame it on "being a teenager"

Five Reasons It Sucks to Be a Teenager

1. You're not an adult
2. Your earlier-than-everybody-else's curfew
3. There are 365 days in a year and almost half of them are school days
4. Homework
5. These four little words: "Because I said so"

When you were born, your parents read stacks of books, watched videos, and got tons of advice on raising children. But you got squat about how to handle *them*. That was fine when all you really needed was a few good meals and a regular diaper change, but now things are different (even though you could still use a good meal). Just like they relied on *What to Expect When You're Expecting*, you need some advice on how to survive the fights, earn their trust, and get them to treat you like an adult.

Let's face it: Parents should come with an instruction booklet. What if the cable guy just dropped your dish off on the doorstep without giving you any directions or help? You wouldn't have a clue how to hook it up, much less actually get it working. It's the same with your parents. Without instructions, how are you supposed to know what makes them tick and which buttons will totally set them off? What tools do you need to fix them when they break down or when things between you get rusty? And once you get things running smoothly, what do you need to do to keep them that way? Consider this book a crash course in raising your parents. It's the all-inclusive guide the "cable guy" forgot to drop off, with countless

tips for decoding your parents, developing a good relationship with them (yes, it's possible), and keeping things running smoothly.

When I was a teenager, my need to be an individual kept me at constant odds with my parents. We fought about curfews, boyfriends, whether my shorts were too short, my shirts too low, my grades too average, and everything in between. They were always hounding me about how much gas I'd left in the family car or telling me I needed to stop being so moody. (*Moody* was their favorite word for about three years—hearing it still makes me nauseous.) A parental instruction book would've seriously made my life easier or at least saved me from some of those late night "We Know Best" discussions.

I'm not trying to bash my parents; I was far from the perfect teenager. There was the time I fell asleep watching stupid British comedy reruns at a guy-friend's house and got home $3^1/2$ hours late for my curfew. I knew I was in deep when I pulled up to the house and the light in my parents' bedroom was still on. I didn't even stop to take off my shoes when I walked through the front door. I went straight to their room, heart pounding, and started to make excuses. Let's just say it wasn't pretty. I was grounded for so long, and I didn't see my guy friend—or anyone else for that matter—for weeks. (And I know my parents still think I was up to no good, even though I was sound asleep on the couch. I swear.)

Then there was the time that news of my "small" birthday party spread around the entire tenth grade and almost 500 people showed up at my house to celebrate. I was worried that there wasn't enough cake, but my parents were freaking about people parking on the grass and making a mess of the basement. I guess I can relate a little, but come on, grass grows back and my friends and I picked everything up. Why couldn't they just relax and enjoy the party?

Why are parents so protective? Sure, they love you, but can't they stop worrying for at least one Friday night? Are they really that scared of you growing up? In a word, yes. For your parents, the thought of you driving, when just a few years ago you could hardly ride a bike, is totally overwhelming. They just barely taught you to look both ways when crossing the street. How can you already be dating and making college plans? Before you start raising your parents, remember that they are as new to this as you are. They mean well, but they're totally clueless (and not in the Alicia Silverstone way). Even if they've had teenagers before, they've never had to deal with you as a teenager, and they desperately need help adjusting to the fact that you're suddenly capable of handling some things on your own. It's a new ball game, so don't be hard on them. Well, not *too* hard, you'll want to give them a little run for their money.

Happy reading!

—Sarah

Chapter **ONE**

Parent
Profiles

Before you can actually start raising your parents, you have to decide which categories they fall into. Think of it as figuring out which table they'd be sitting at during lunch if they were your age.

Parent: The Hippie

The look: Linen pants, Birkenstocks, and a yoga mat

Nags you about: Talking about your feelings, spending time with the family

Parental catchphrase: "How do you feel about that?"

Hobbies: Listening to NPR, watching BBC news, gardening

Favorite magazine: Magazines? The Hippie only reads the hard news found in the *New York Times*.

Favorite form of teen torture: Family "meetings" to talk about your problems

Famous celebrity counterparts: John Lennon and Yoko Ono

How to Spot This Parent: The Hippie's favorite hangout is, you guessed it, Whole Foods. Where else can the Hippie find organic granola, free-range chicken, and shade-grown coffee in one-stop shopping?

Your Best Bet for Getting Out of Trouble: It's rare for the Hippie to totally lose it, so when he freaks, you need to take it seriously. Apologize ASAP and ask what you can do to help. Hippies love helping hands.

Parent: **The Schoolmarm**

The look: High-waisted pleated trousers and thick glasses

Nags you about: Grades, ACT/SAT scores, your college aspirations, when you're late for school

Parental catchphrase: "Algebra is easy. If I did it, you can do it."

Hobbies: Doing a crossword puzzle, watching *Jeopardy*

Favorite magazine: *Scientific American*

Favorite form of teen torture: Barring all TV for extended periods of time

Famous celebrity counterpart: Principal Skinner, from *The Simpsons*

How to Spot This Parent: It's no surprise that the Schoolmarm often can be found with her nose in a book or wandering around the local art museum. Another determining feature is that slightly dazed expression this parent gets when deep in thought.

Your Best Bet for Getting Out of Trouble: Grades are always on the Schoolmarm's mind, so when you find yourself in deep with this parent, try to bring the focus back to school; promising to study more and get good grades will help defuse a lot of fights.

Parent: The Teen Wannabe

The look: Miniskirts, stilettos, and sticky lip gloss

Nags you about: Whom you're dating, whom your friends are dating, the latest school gossip

Parental catchphrase: "That is so wack."

Hobbies: Shopping, going to the gym, listening to pop music

Favorite magazine: *Cosmopolitan*

Favorite form of teen torture: Grounding you for life

Famous celebrity counterpart: Pamela Anderson (Hello, cover up that cleavage!)

How to Spot This Parent: The Teen Wannabe often can be seen working it on the elliptical machine at the gym. She will be completely made up and likely wearing a pink-velour sweat suit. Other favorite locales are the mall and local nail salon.

Your Best Bet for Getting Out of Trouble: Since the Teen Wannabe is known for flying off the handle and handing out some over-the-top punishments (e.g., threatening to install a GPS in your car), you've got to keep your cool if you don't want the threats to stick.

Parent: The Yuppie

The look: A mature J.Crew model with graying hair

Nags you about: What colleges you get into, how many hours a day you spend on the computer

Parental catchphrase: "If you're going to get into Princeton . . ."

Hobbies: Golf, tennis, and reading the *Wall Street Journal*

Favorite magazine: *Travel + Leisure*

Favorite form of teen torture: Taking away your allowance

Famous celebrity counterparts: Most politicians. Just look for the collared polo shirt.

How to Spot This Parent: The Yuppie is known to frequent the local Starbucks and can be overheard ordering a "grande, half-caff, no-foam, one-shot-of-vanilla latte." Whew! It's hard work being the Yuppie.

Your Best Bet for Getting Out of Trouble: The Yuppie appreciates a well-thought-out argument. Present your side of the argument and take the punishment like an adult—your parent will respect you for it.

Parent: The Sibling Activist

The look: Beware—this parent can look like anyone!

Nags you about: Your little brother's every want and need, when you borrow your sister's jeans without asking

Parental catchphrase: "Can't you be more like your older sister?"

Hobbies: Talking about your siblings to anyone who will listen

Favorite magazine: *Parents*, of course

Favorite form of teen torture: Letting your older brother take the car, even when you already have plans with your BFF.

Famous celebrity counterpart: The Simpson sisters' father and manager, Joe Simpson. Everybody knows he likes Jessica better than Ashlee.

How to Spot This Parent: Look for the Sibling Activist at your brother's hockey game, karate class, and debate tournament. Where the favorite child goes, the Sibling Activist goes.

Your Best Bet for Getting Out of Trouble: If your parent is a true Sibling Activist, then it's likely that a fight will be blamed on you and not your sister. It sucks, but if you want to come out of fights unscathed, don't blame anyone else, especially your little brother.

Parent: **The Total Control Freak**

The look: Perfectly ironed collars and a perfect smile

Nags you about: Your latest physics test score, how much time you spend on your cell phone, chewing gum, talking with your mouth full, how your shirt doesn't match those shoes, how you're spending too much time with your friends, how you aren't being a good friend, how you answer your phone by saying "yeah"

Parental catchphrase: "I need to know where you're going, who you're going with, and when you're going to be home."

Hobbies: PTA, Book Club, throwing dinner parties

Favorite magazine: *Martha Stewart Living* (duh)

Favorite form of teen torture: Calling your cell every ten minutes to check in

Famous celebrity counterpart: Martha Stewart

How to Spot This Parent: You have to be quick on your feet to spot the Total Control Freak. This parent is busy buzzing from work to after-school activities, the grocery store, and everywhere else. After all, the Total Control Freak likes to do everything herself because she does it correctly.

Your Best Bet for Getting Out of Trouble: When the Total Control Freak is angry, you'd best lay low until things blow over. She's got so much going on that she doesn't have much patience, and if you push her too far, you'll be the one who pays for it.

Lost in Translation
Still trying to figure out which types of parents you have? Take this quiz to figure it out.

1. You walk downstairs in a denim miniskirt, but before you get out the front door, your mom looks you over and says . . .

A. You are not going to school wearing that.

B. Um, have a good day at school, honey.

C. Love the skirt. Do you want to borrow my silver clogs to wear with it?

2. Your school calls to say that you were absent from geometry class today. After he hangs up the phone, your dad turns to you and says . . .

A. I don't care if your best friend's dog died. There's no excuse for missing school.

B. That was your school. Did something happen today? They said you missed geometry.

C. I remember skipping math with my best friend, Allen. Man, we hated our teacher.

3. You come home 25 minutes late for curfew, but you haven't been late in over six months. When you open the door, your parent says . . .

A. Where have you been? I've been pacing around, wondering whether or not to call the police!
B. I know you haven't been late in a while, but that doesn't make it OK this time. Be sure you're home on time tomorrow.
C. Twenty-five minutes late, huh? Did Justin kiss you at the door?

4. You get cut during basketball tryouts, even though you really should've made the team. You're sitting in the kitchen totally ripping on the coach for being blind, and your mom says . . .
A. I'm calling that coach. If that Johnson kid is on the team, you should be on the team.
B. I'm so sorry you didn't make it. No wonder you're upset.
C. This sucks. Let's go get a Jamba Juice and forget about the team.

5. You forget to pick up your sister and her friends from the mall and instead check out the latest Jake Gyllenhaal flick with your crush. You get home after the movie and your sister starts yelling that you left her there on purpose. Your dad gets between the two of you and says . . .
A. I hope that movie was worth it. You're grounded! And no cell phone either!
B. It's not like you to forget your sister. How are you going to make it up to her?
C. OK, OK. Enough fighting. Tell your sister you're sorry, and let's drop it.

6. You never swear, but one afternoon you're clearing out the dishwasher and you drop a china plate. It shatters, and the word "sh*#" slips out of your mouth. Your mom's jaw falls open, and she says . . .
A. I'm not going to have you swearing in my house!
B. Nothing. Just raises an eyebrow and gives you a ten-second stare.
C. What the hell?

7. You got into a little fender bender in the school parking lot. Your bumper isn't bad, but the other driver's needs to be replaced. You call your dad at work, and he says . . .
A. I told you not to talk on your phone while driving. This is coming out of your allowance!
B. Are you hurt? How bad is it?
C. It was the other kid's fault, wasn't it?

Answers:

Mostly As: The Fly-Off-the-Handle Parent (aka the Yuppie, the Sibling Activist, the Total Control Freak)

Expect this parent to freak out at almost everything and you won't be caught off guard the next time he starts yelling that you're late for curfew. This parent means well but can't seem to keep calm, even when the smallest thing happens (like you getting a B- on your math quiz. Hello, a B-?). But the fly-off-the-handle parent has a hard time seeing reason.

In order to cope and keep the yelling to a minimum, you'll have to be the one to keep your cool. When your parents start screaming about the pile of laundry sitting on your bedroom floor, take a deep breath and offer a solution. Would a laundry basket help keep things organized? What if you get the mess cleaned up by the end of the week? Dirty laundry isn't the end of the world so be sure you don't act like it (even if your parent does). Your calmness will probably wear off on your mom or dad, and if nothing else, at least you'll be Zen.

Mostly Bs: The Choose-My-Battles Parent (aka the Hippie, the Schoolmarm)

Consider yourself lucky. Sure, your parent isn't perfect, but give her a little credit—she doesn't flip out over every little thing and generally gets you. This parent tends to be slightly overprotective but has moments of utter coolness, like that time she let you and your friends take the Suburban out at 2:00 AM to toilet paper your ex-boyfriend's house. Plus, your friends probably think your parent is pretty cool, even if he's not perfect. You probably feel sometimes that this parent pries a little and wants you to open up about personal things, but it could be worse. . . .

Mostly Cs: The I'm-Trying-Too-Hard Parent (aka the Teen Wannabe)

This parent is also known as the Wannabe Parent. Sure it's nice to have your parent take your side most of the time, but don't you wish she weren't always trying so hard to be your friend? You do want a parent, after all. You've got plenty of friends your age, and isn't your parent supposed to be the adult? While this parent may be good to have around for going to the latest chick flick or shopping for a new back-to-school wardrobe, it's a pain to have a parent who keeps flipping back and forth between cool-with-anything friend and I'm-the-boss-of-you adult. It can be hard to keep your parent-teen relationship balanced, but if you treat your parent like a parent (i.e. don't let your mom borrow your miniskirts and try to listen when she's talking to you), chances are she'll start acting like a parent.

A few of all three: The "Normal" Parent (a combination of two or more of the different parental breeds)

Most teenagers in the world live with the Normal Parent. You never know what to expect from this parent. (And your parent probably thinks he never knows what to expect from you.) Sometimes, when you expect your parent to flip, she's calm and shrugs it off. Then something will happen that you think is no big deal, and your parent freaks. Welcome to the world of parents. It's full of surprises—some good, some bad. The one thing you can count on is that even though you love each other, you're not always going to agree. So keep your cool and know when to stick to your guns and when to back down—the basics of a happy relationship with your parents, or anyone else.

"It is not a bad thing that children should occasionally, and politely, put parents in their place."
—Sidonie Gabrielle Colette, French novelist

Chapter TWO

Let's Get Together—
The Art of Negotiation

Picture yourself as a big lawyer—a smarter, parent-savvy version of Reese Witherspoon's character in *Legally Blonde*. Whenever you ask your parents for money or to borrow the family car, you're in the courthouse. If Mom wants you to clean the attic before you go to the movies, you're on the courtroom floor. When Dad says the two of you need to talk about your latest report card, you're standing in front of the jury giving your closing statement. One of a lawyer's main jobs is to mediate between clients and come to an agreement to satisfy both parties. In this situation, your parents are the other clients. How can you make a successful case with them on the other side of the table? It's all about negotiation, baby.

Good negotiation skills are key for dealing with parents. You don't want every discussion to turn into a fight, but you can't just give in to all their demands either. How can you talk them into getting you a cell phone? What can you do if your dad says you're not leaving the house dressed like that? The right negotiation tactics will save you a lot of stress and a lot of screaming. (And hey, they might even come in handy when you really are a big-shot lawyer.)

The first step to winning your case is research. Lawyers spend most of their time behind the scenes, figuring out what the other side is going to bring to the table and what they are willing to walk away with. And just like a lawyer, you have to come to the court-room anticipating what your parents are going to say and calculating your responses. Take a few minutes to step into your parents' shoes. If you understand their perspective, you'll all start off on the right foot. And your parents will be more likely to respect your perspective if it's clear you've taken time to understand theirs.

If you've considered the case from all angles and still feel like you have a good argument, then let the negotiations begin.

Bargaining Basics
10 Things to Remember for Every Negotiation

1. Some things just aren't negotiable.
It doesn't matter what a good bargainer you are if you're asking your parents for something ridiculous. You could negotiate for years and never convince them to buy you the MINI Cooper you've been lusting over. So remember to keep your expectations realistic. Do you know any parent who would send her teenage daughter on an all-expenses-paid trip to Cancun with three of her best friends and no parents? Didn't think so, don't even ask.

2. Prove yourself.
Good luck trying to get your dad to hand over the car keys if the last time you borrowed his wheels you were late for curfew and left him with an empty tank. He's no fool. Why should he think this time will be any different? But, say last time you borrowed the car you got home on time and left a few bucks for gas in the cup holder. (Bonus points if you actually went to the gas station and squeegeed

the windows while you filled up.) You'd have shown that you respect him and his car. He'll have a hard time finding a good reason for not giving you the keys if you've earned them.

3. Timing is everything.

You are dying to get some cash for a new prom dress (hello, prom is less than a month away), and you're planning to ask your dad when he gets home from work. When he walks through the door, he announces that he just got a speeding ticket. Hint: Now is probably not the best time to ask—for anything. Your dad is pissed about being pulled over, and if you put one more thing on him (even if it is just a prom dress), he's probably totally going to flip. Do yourself (and your dad) a favor and wait until the speeding ticket trauma has worn off a little before asking for some dress dough.

4. Be clear about what you want and need.

It sounds obvious, but sometimes you really have to spell out what you're asking for in order for your parents to understand. Sure, they get that you want a cell phone, but do they know why? Remember, they aren't mind readers. Tell them that cell phones are how your generation communicates, that you feel safer if you have one when you're driving, and you think it will help them keep track of you. The more information you give your parents, the better they'll understand you.

5. Give a little, get a little.

Parents don't like ultimatums, and they probably won't stand for one. "If you don't let me stay over at Emily's, I'm never babysitting for you again" isn't the most effective way to get your butt to Emily's. Instead, try giving your parents a few options: If they let you stay at Emily's tonight, you'll babysit for them on Saturday. Or, since they won't let you stay at Emily's tonight, what about letting you spend the night next weekend? The more options you give, the more reasonable you sound, and the better chance you have at actually ending up at Emily's.

6. Tune in.

It seems like the easiest thing in the world, but sometimes just listening to what your parents have to say is the trick to keeping a discussion from turning into a yelling match. You want your parents to listen to you, so in return you owe them the respect of listening to their side of things. They might actually have some good points, but you'll never know if you tune them out.

7. Keep your cool.

Sounds simple enough, but when you're in the throes of a major argument, spouting off about how lame your parents are is like kissing your later curfew good-bye. Instead, focus on telling them how you feel, and don't insult them personally. It sounds like Dr. Phil, but the more you say things like, "This makes me feel angry," or "I feel confused," the more you sound like you're willing to accept responsibility for yourself, and the less defensive your parents will be. You'll never see a top lawyer sobbing or screaming in front of the jury. So when it's time to talk it out with Mom and Dad, check your emotions at the door.

8. Give credit where credit is due.

If you really want your parents to hear you, you have to treat them like real people. I know. I know. Sometimes they seem like they're from another planet, but if you treat your parents as you would like to be treated, you might be surprised. Respect is a two-way street.

9. Don't think of your negotiation as a win/lose situation.

After a two-hour talk about whether you can take the car to the beach or up the canyon for a bonfire, your parents decide you can go only if someone else drives. Don't totally despair. You might not be taking your sweet ride, but at least you can still go to the party. If you make every situation all or nothing, you're never going to be happy. When your parents do give in, say thanks and make the best of it.

10. Breathe.

People don't suggest counting to ten for nothing. Even if you've got a great comeback, take a few deep breaths and consider your response before shouting something out. The more in control you are, the more rational and mature you'll seem, and the more likely your parents are to listen to you.

Mayday! Mayday!

When you're negotiating, keep your ears open for any of these phrases. They're major red flags that your negotiations are headed south!

Boundaries: When they bring up boundaries, chances are your parents are about to set some serious limits on you. Change the topic ASAP!

Rules: According to your parents, rules are NOT meant to be broken. If they bring rules up in the conversation, they're probably about to enforce new ones. If you're already stuck in a rules discussion, it's probably because you've broken one. It happens. To avoid getting hammered with any new restrictions, remind your parents that you know their house rules by giving a quick recap of the main ones—you'll be home in time for curfew, you won't hang at Jessica's if her parents aren't home, and all that jazz. They won't have time to make new rules if you're busy talking about the ones that already exist!

Responsibility: The favorite word of parents everywhere. The best way to fight this one is to bring up legitimate ways you are responsible. Getting straight As? Now would be the perfect time to remind your parents.

Lesson (as in "learn your lesson"): Parents pull this one out when they want to make you learn something the hard way. The hard way is never a good way. Never.

The Write Way to Keep from Losing Your Cool

If you're worried you might not be able to say how you really feel but want your parents to understand where you're coming from, call on the power of the pen and write a letter. You're guaranteed to get your point across, and you won't risk losing the fight because you got all worked up. Not only that, but sometimes when things are written down they seem more serious. Your parents will probably really think about your side of the issue because you've taken so much time to put your feelings out there. And maybe they'll take a cue from you and consider their response before making a decision.

Writing can be a total stress reliever, too. Think of all those times your parents wouldn't let you go out with your friends and you wanted to tell someone how unfair it was. That's when journaling comes in handy. Whether it's on your MySpace blog or in the notebook you keep under your bed, sometimes writing down your private feelings is all you need to get over losing an argument.

A Tip From Someone Who's Been There

"Every parent I know gets super pissed when they see their teenager roll her eyes. It's basically like you're telling them to screw off, but not in so many words. Hey, I know sometimes eye-rolling can be second nature, but if you want to keep Mom in a good mood, skip it. No one wants to be told to screw off. Not even you." —Lucy, 24

Chapter **THREE**

Leave Me Alone—
How to Get Some Privacy

Ever heard Aretha Franklin sing "Respect"? That girl knew what she was singing about. Now if only your parents would show a little respect and give you some privacy. But ask them to give you some space or say you want to be alone, and the teen tragedy featured on last night's news starts blaring in their heads. Parents think because you want some privacy it means you're seriously depressed or dealing drugs out your bedroom window. (They're your parents, remember. They worry about you!) But wanting privacy doesn't mean you're up to no good.

That's when trust enters the equation. Before you can expect your parents to give you a little space, you have to prove you deserve their trust. So what's the best way to get trustworthy status? Simple honesty. If your parents know you're going to be honest with them, they'll come right to you when they're worried about something. And even though dealing with them straight-up might stress you out, it's actually a compliment that your parents think you're grown-up enough to handle an adult conversation. It's all about the respect. Sing it, Aretha.

Parents Talk Back

"In my mind, trust is like a bank account. When my teenager is honest with me, the trust account is full and the leash is loose, but when she makes withdrawals from the trust account, the trust balance goes down and the leash grows tighter. It is possible to refill the account with frequent and consistent deposits to the account. When I say, 'you just made a huge withdrawal from the trust account,' my kids know exactly what that means. If only they understood that a full trust account means almost total freedom!" —Julie, 50

Knock Knock
Keys to Keeping Your Private Space Private

Even though your parents are paying the mortgage, your room should be your own little sanctuary. A place you can go to escape from school, your parents, and anything else that is about to send you over the edge. How nice would it be to completely lock the outside world out for a little while? But no, your parents aren't havin' it.

When you ask about getting a lock on your door, your parents immediately ask, "What are you hiding in there?" The answer to this, of course, is "nothing." But your parents won't go for that. You need to explain exactly why you don't want anyone coming in your room—your sister steals your clothes, people barge in when you're getting dressed, and you need somewhere you can go to get away every once in a while.

If your parents won't budge and it looks like you're doomed to having an open-door policy forever, try a compromise tactic. Ask that every time anyone in the family wants to come in, they knock and wait for you to say it's OK to enter. And make it clear that if you aren't there, the room is off-limits. While this might not guarantee that your younger brother won't try to sneak in to listen to your iPod when you're out with your friends, it should give you some more "me time"—you know, for the important private things you have to do, like putting on your pants.

What to Do When All Else Fails:
The Trash Tactic (Use at Your Own Risk)

By the looks of it, a lot of guys I dated in high school were trying the trash tactic. Their rooms were so nasty that no one (not even them) wanted to go in there. No mom or dad wants to spend hours digging through piles of dirty clothes, smelly socks, and half-eaten bags of Cheetos. And while it's not a good way to make friends, it does guarantee a sort of de facto privacy.

The downside? Storing up that much dirty laundry isn't easy or fun. Plus, you're just asking for some extra chores when your Mom catches a whiff from underneath your door.

Parental Ruse Rating: B+

When Mom or Dad Goes Too Far

Just because you've earned your parents' trust doesn't mean they won't be tempted to stray every once in a while. When it comes to basic privacy, know that if you leave something out, your parents will read it. I used to have a running joke with my friend Jed about "getting it on" in the student-body office—not a joke my parents would have appreciated. One day when he was bored in Spanish, Jed wrote me a note and said I should meet him after school for our "rendezvous." That night, I accidentally left the note sitting next to my bathroom sink. The next morning I walked into the bathroom and found my dad reading every word. Since when does leaving a note on the counter make it public property?

I hadn't learned the first and most important rule in privacy maintenance: Don't leave a paper trail. (See rule details below.) In the end, my dad dropped the whole incident, but he never really liked Jed again. And you'd better believe that was the last time I left a note sitting around, even the ones that said, "You look cute today."

When it comes to privacy, you can learn a few things from spies. We're not talking international espionage here, just some helpful tricks you can pick up without having to join the secret service or go through basic intelligence training.

Spy Secrets

1. Don't leave a paper trail.
Remember my story about Jed? A good spy and a smart teen won't leave her personal e-mail open on the computer or leave a note sitting on the kitchen counter. Your parents may think they're full-on adults, but tempt them with something from your personal life and they're like kids in a candy store. If you leave something out, they're going to read it. No matter what it says. Don't make it that easy for them to invade your privacy.

2. Don't lie—ever.
Honesty is the key to respect, remember? And respect equals more privacy. In general, spies tell as few lies as possible because it's too hard to remember all the complicated details of a story that isn't

true. Good spies keep it simple because they know they're bound to get caught in their own lies. But not lying doesn't mean you have to spill all your private details to your parents. You can keep some things personal and still be honest with them. That's where rule #3 comes in.

3. Remember that some things don't need to be out in the open.

Spies don't have a problem keeping secrets that are essential to their mission. Remember that your mission is to make it out of high school unscathed. There's nothing wrong with keeping conversations between friends private, whether they take place over e-mail, on the phone, or in texts. If your parents ask about something you don't want to discuss, tell them why. Explain that Rachel's having trouble with her boyfriend but that you don't want to break her trust by spilling the details. Your parents will probably respect your loyalty and will likely feel better once they know you aren't keeping secrets to hide something. Most parents don't care if Alex kissed Liz last night or that Jessica failed her English test. They're asking questions to make sure things are OK with you.

4. Don't be paranoid.

If your dad asks what you did last night, he's probably just trying to have a conversation with you. He just wants to be part of your life. Any spy will tell you it's a mistake to act defensive when you don't have anything to be defensive about. Sometimes it's annoying to come home to a million questions, but totally shutting your parents out will make them suspicious, even when they don't have any reason to be.

Parental Spyware

Chances are, you probably aren't the only one using spy techniques. A lot of parents are installing parental spyware on family computers so they can track everything that happens on the Internet. Even though there are different kinds of software, most programs offer the same basic services. For example, if your parents have installed spyware on your computer, they can probably see how many IMs you send, who you send them to, and maybe even read them! And that's not all, most spyware also makes it possible to count the number of e-mails you send and receive and will report any Web sites you've visited in the last few days. The lesson here? Simple—don't do anything stupid online.

What do you do if you catch your mom or dad rummaging through your room or trying to break into your e-mail?

A. Decide you're never going to e-mail, write in your diary, text message, or anything else for the rest of your life.

B. Buy a one-way ticket to anywhere because you're so mad you can't even think about talking to them ever again.

C. Tell your parents you plan to go through their mail, e-mail, and any other personal items since that's what they did to you.

before you take a deep breath and do the following. (Hint: This is your best bet.)

After you calm down from the initial shock of having your parents invade your trust and personal space, you need to have a major talk with them. It sounds awful, but if you don't talk things out, your anger and resentment will just get worse. And that means your relationship will just get worse. Remember, they are your parents and, technically, are in charge of you for at least another few years. (And they have the keys to the car.)

Time Warp

When your mom and dad were teenagers, they only had to worry about their parents reading their diaries and private notes. MySpace, e-mail, text messages, and IMs weren't even part of the picture! With all this new technology, it's even more important to have a house rule: if it's not addressed to you, don't read it. Your parents would've died if their mom or dad read their diary entries, so why should they expect you to be OK when they snoop in your e-mail or check your cell phone for old texts? It's the same thing.

Before you ask them, ask yourself if you've done something to break their trust. Do they have a reason to be concerned for your safety or well-being? Step into their shoes for a minute. What could make them worry enough to snoop through your stuff? If you haven't done anything wrong and you don't think they have a good reason to be snooping around, you have every right to be mad that your privacy was violated. When you are ready to talk, explain exactly what they did to make you feel violated, and ask them why they felt the need to go through your things. Being open and discussing things calmly will help dispel their concerns. Once you and your parents have gotten everything out in the open, you need to figure out how you're going to deal with their intrusion. Are they going to respect your privacy in the future? Will they promise to talk to you first if they're concerned instead of going straight for your cell phone?

Let's face it. Your parents aren't going to stop worrying about you. (It's part of their job description.) So you have to figure out a solution that works for all of you for when they start to overreact about your grades or your new motorcycle-driving boyfriend—and it's not going through your closet.

Just Being a Normal Teenager

On top of being trustworthy, part of getting privacy is demanding privacy and being willing to negotiate for it. (Chapter 2, anyone?) In a lot of situations, your parents are holding the cards—they're the ones who make the rules after all. To tip the scales in your favor, you need to know how to talk things out and make your parents see things from your point of view. That means staying calm and making a case for yourself. When my friend Eric was 15, he had to do just that:

"My parents said I was surly and withdrawn (and I was), but they were positive I was on drugs (and I wasn't). Seriously, just because you hate your math teacher or listen to punk music doesn't mean you're getting high."

Eric's parents started to make jokes about getting him drug tested. It became obvious they weren't completely kidding when they started threatening to take him to the doctor.

"I wasn't on drugs. In fact, I'd never even seen drugs. But I felt really violated and angry that my parents wouldn't trust me. I wasn't doing anything wrong, just being a normal teenager."

Eric was pissed, but he didn't freak out right away. He thought about yelling at his parents, and he considered refusing to take the test, but he didn't want the drug-test threat looming for the rest of his high-school years. In the end, Eric used his innocence to outsmart his parents.

"I knew I would pass the drug test. So the next time it came up, I looked my parents in the eyes and said, 'I'll take your test, but when I pass it, I want a new mountain bike.' They never mentioned it again."

Even though Eric didn't get the new bike, he won the battle and some respect. Score one for the teenager!

Chapter **FOUR**

Planet Teen—Hip Hop, Hanging Out, and Your Entourage

You know that look your parents give you when you come into the kitchen wearing green eye shadow or when you ask for a later curfew because it's your annual *Sex and the City* marathon with your best friend? The look that says, "you MUST be from a different planet." Sometimes it seems like you're worlds away from each other. But if you're going to get your parents to respect your tunes, your friends, and your love life, you've got to bring them to Planet Teen for a while.

Hanging Out
(aka Undercover Dating)

If Charles Darwin were alive and studying teen evolution, he would be impressed. After generations of parents freaking out when their teenagers went on dates, the teen population got smart and started saying they were "hanging out." This is definitely a good thing because when it comes to the opposite sex, the word *date* is like a bright red flag. The thought of you hitting the town with someone who might kiss you (or worse!) sends your parents into a state of total panic. To a parent's ears, "hanging out" sounds much safer than "dating." Go with this.

Another essential trick for undercover dating is to know how to label your crush.

Don't call him your boyfriend until you absolutely have to. *Boyfriend* is another warning word for parents. Instead, call him your "guy friend" or this "guy I kind of like." Don't give your parents a reason to flip if there isn't one!

But, significant other or not, your parents are never going to be completely comfortable with you dating. What are they so scared of? Let's be frank. They're freaked that something—any-thing—bad is going to happen: that you'll get pregnant, get an STD, or get taken advantage of. Sounds pretty dramatic right? But when you consider the scary stats of teen pregnancy and rape, your parents have legitimate reasons to be worried. So instead of trying to convince them that you aren't going to be the next teen pregnancy disaster (which, of course, you aren't), you have to prove to your parents that they can trust you and the people you're going out with.

Since When Does a Date Include Your Dad?

"I'll never forget when, on my first date with this really hot guy, we rented a movie and took it back to my house. My dad didn't think our flick was 'appropriate for teenagers,' so he sat and watched the entire thing with us! After an agonizing $2^1/2$ hours, the movie was finally over. I walked the guy to my front door with my dad listening from the other room. All I could mutter was 'Thanks for the movie,' before I shut the door. Then, when I got back to the family room, my dad said, 'That was fun.' The nerve! Needless to say, that guy never called again." —Sarah, 16

Operation Safe Dating
Four Ways to Prove You're Dating-Dependable

1. Let your parents meet the people you go out with. We're not talking a sit-down interview before you can leave the house, just a quick, "Hello, I promise to take good care of your daughter," introduction.

2. Tell your parents what you'll do on the date. If they have a general idea of what you and your date are up to, they're less likely to freak when they catch you kissing on the porch or you get home five minutes late.

3. When you come in from a date, stop in your parents' room to say good-night and offer them a tidbit about the date. Something like, "The movie totally sucked," or "We had the best banana splits at that new ice-cream place on Main Street"—any little thing to let them know you weren't making out the entire night. (Plus, they love having some insider info on your life.)

4. If your parents can't stand the idea of you dating one-on-one, then go out on group dates. You can still sit by your crush at the movie, flirt at a party, and generally feel like you're on a date, even if you're with a few friends.

Getting Too Serious

If getting your parents to be cool about dating lots of people isn't a problem, chances are your parents are on your case about "getting too serious." You're crazy about this guy, but your parents worry that you're limiting yourself by dating just one person. To top it off, they don't think he's good enough for you.

The first step to breaking in that special someone is to have him spend some time at your house. Sounds like the absolute worst thing to do, right? But it's like reverse therapy. Your parents aren't going to like a guy they don't know, so give them a chance to get to know why you're totally crushing on Mr. Adorable. They'll probably like the fact that he's on the soccer team or is super into his art. They have to give him a chance if he's willing to suffer through a family dinner or play cards on a Sunday night. And after spending some time with them, your boyfriend will probably think your family is cool—just one more reason you're such a catch!

Parents Too Judgmental? You're Not Alone . . .

"My parents never like the guys I date. In fact, they find every possible opportunity to bombard me with advice, and they never fail to add snide little comments, even when they are completely irrelevant. I was walking down the street with my mom, and we saw this sketchy looking man. You could tell he was trouble. My mom leaned over to me and commented, 'If you date a slouch, you'll marry a slouch.' I was taken aback and totally offended. How in any way was this sketchy man related to my boyfriend? (And since when am I thinking about getting married?) Just because my guy doesn't wear a suit and tie to school doesn't mean he's trashy. He's good to me, all my friends like him, and he's making serious college plans. Hardly a slouch, but just try convincing my mom."

—Alison, 18

If you're going to have your latest crush hanging out at the house, you're probably going to be making out at your house. And let's be honest, even though there's nothing wrong with kissing, who wants their parents walking in while you're engaged in lip-lock with that cute guy from Spanish class? Here are a few tried-and-true tricks for happy in-house dating.

1. Set the ground rules before the game starts. In other words, talk to your parents about having your crush over before it actually happens. Will they let you watch the movie with the door closed? How late is your date allowed to stay? And are they really going to leave you alone or is house-hanging basically the same as family time? This is where your negotiation skills are key. Be prepared to give and take a little, but remind your parents that they'd probably rather have you and McHottie chilling at your house than somewhere else.

2. No matter what room you're making out in, keep the lights on. Parents freak when you're chillin' in the dark—even if you're in the family room. Plus, if it's dark, they're more likely to check on you.

3. If you're downstairs, listen for their footsteps. A sure sign they're on the way to make sure everything is, you know, parent approved.

4. If you get caught with lips locked, be cool. Take a break from making out and go to the kitchen to get a snack or soda. You probably feel like disappearing into the floor, but the more calm you are, the more calm your date and your parents will be. Chances are, even your parents will understand your embarrassment and cut you a break.

Undercover Makeout Session . . . Uncovered!

"Once, we were in the basement, waiting for an opportunity to kiss but not forgetting the lurking presence of my parents upstairs. We knew that after someone came downstairs, we had a little while before we were interrupted again. After my brother came down to check up on us, we figured the coast was clear, so you can imagine our surprise when my dad snuck up on us during a full-on make-out sesh and asked us what we were watching. Duh, obviously there wasn't much watching going on. Mortified, we separated, and my dad said it was time to call it a night. Unfortunately, the worst part was not over. I had to face 'the council' (aka my parents). After bidding good-night to my boyfriend with a nod of my head, I went up to my bedroom and waited to be summoned. My dad wasted no time filling my mom in on the events, and I was soon called to their room to find them perched on the bed, ready. It was a game of 2-on-1. After suffering through a twenty-minute lecture of how 'inappropriate' it was for me to be full-on making out with a guy like that, I was dismissed, but that wasn't the end of it. Now my boyfriend can barely even face my dad, and I'm terrified to even hug him at my house. I can't imagine what my parents would have done if we would have been doing anything more than kissing!" —Lizzie, 18

What If Boys Aren't the Issue?

What if instead of fantasizing about that built guy on swim team, your McDreamy is the hot girl in AP chem?

Surprise! You're attracted to girls. Is that the end of the world? No. Will your parents think it's the end of the world? Maybe. So what are you going to tell them?

When it comes right down to it, you don't have to share your sexual identity with your parents (or anyone else) until you're ready. It is your sexual identity, after all. But you might feel like, in order to really be yourself, you need to be up front with your parents from the get-go. It can be really scary to have this conversation since every parent is different and relationships can be an uncomfortable topic. And while there's no perfect strategy for starting a discussion, here are a few things to keep in mind when you finally decide to sit down and spill it to your parents.

1. Communication is now more important than ever.
Ask your parents to let you share your feelings and then give them space to share theirs. They might not like what you have to say (and you might not like what they have to say either), but if you're ever going to be on the same page, you'll all have to keep open minds. Everyone needs to check preconceived notions at the door.

Try to see things from your parents' points of view. If your parents freak out when you come out, chances are it's partly because their vision of your life includes a husband, house in the suburbs, and 2.5 kids. They'll need some time to adjust that vision. You might also have to help them see that being a lesbian doesn't mean that you're going to be shunned from society or have limited opportunities. Times have changed and are still changing.

2. Explain to your parents that just because you're attracted to girls doesn't mean you've changed.
You're still the same person you were before you decided to open up to them—the same daughter who likes flavored lip gloss, sings in the shower, and grew up playing with Bratz. Tell them how much their support means to you; they are your parents after all, and you've relied on them for everything from diapers to driver's licenses. You don't want that to change now.

3. Recognize that your parents might have questions and concerns.
Be prepared to offer them information on where they can turn to get their questions answered. The following organizations can help with all the uncertainty they (and you) might be feeling:

• Parents, Families, and Friends of Lesbians and Gays (PFLAG), **www.pflag.org**. PFLAG is a national not-for-profit organization that offers support, education, and advocacy for gay people and their families and friends. There are local chapters of PFLAG around the country, and most of them have regular meetings that are open to the public.

• The Lesbian, Gay, Bisexual, and Transgender Community Center, **www.gaycenter.org**. Based in New York, the Lesbian, Gay, Bisexual, and Transgender Community Center is the largest LGBT multiservice organization on the East Coast and the second largest in the world. They provide social services, public policy, education, and cultural/recreational programs and support.

4. Do your research.

There are some great organizations dedicated to helping teenagers like you, who are struggling with their sexuality and trying to talk to their parents about it. Your school or local college may have a Gay-Straight Alliance, with people who are going through or have been through exactly what you're dealing with. And on top of local groups, here are some national associations and societies that can help you:

• The Gay and Lesbian National Hotline, **www.glnh.org** and 1-888-THE-GLNH (1-888-843-4564). Offers peer counseling Monday through Friday, between 4:00 PM and midnight, and Saturdays, noon to 5:00 PM Eastern Standard Time.

- Advocates for Youth, **www.advocatesforyouth.org**. Creates programs and advocates for policies that help teenagers make informed and responsible decisions about their sexual and reproductive health.

- The National Coalition for Gay, Lesbian, Bisexual, and Transgender Youth, **www.outproud.org**. Offers support for gay and lesbian youth through advocacy and providing resources and other information.

Chances are, after your parents have some time to adjust, you'll be closer to them than you've ever been. But no matter how they respond, you should be proud of who you are. It takes a lot of guts to open up and be honest with the people you love. One of Shakespeare's most famous lines (from *Hamlet*) is "to thine own self be true." Go Shakespeare!

Dating? What Dating?

You've got a lot going on. Between school, piano, the basketball team, and spending time with your crew, you don't even have time to think about dating much less spend an entire Saturday night out with someone you're not that into.

It's totally OK if there's no one you're interested in or if dating just isn't your thing. But it might not be OK with your parents. What if they're constantly asking about your love life and trying to force their friends' kids on you? (Believe me. Just because your mom says Mrs. Friedman's son is "really cute" doesn't mean it's true.)

You've got to be straight with them. Tell them there's no way you'll ever meet someone you really like if you spend every weekend going out with their "set-ups." Not to mention that's not how you want to spend your time. Reassure them that just because you don't want to date now doesn't mean you never will. For now take the stance that you shouldn't have to date if you don't want to. Period.

Posse Power

Of course, no matter what your dating life is like, you can't live without your entourage. Who else are you supposed to call when your crush finally asks you out or you're stumped by #9 on your geometry homework? But what happens if your parents don't like your friends, or they think you spend too much time together?

Truthfully, your parents don't have to like your friends. They aren't the ones hanging out with them. But do ask yourself why your mom and dad are so against you spending time with Lauren. Do they have a good reason for being worried? Is she trouble with a capital *T*?

If your parents don't have any real reasons not to like your friends (and Abbie's revealing shirts or the fact that Claire doesn't have a curfew ARE NOT legitimate reasons to not like someone), then ask them to give your friends a chance. They can't call your best friend a bad influence if you're on the honor roll and still make your bed every day.

Sometimes your friend problems have nothing to do with your parents disliking your pals. Sometimes your parents get worked up because they think you spend too much time with your posse and not enough with them (and the rest of your family, of course). But, as with all things, it is possible to reach middle ground and get your parents to loosen the reins a little. Try these techniques.

1. Agree on some sort of schedule and stick to it.

This means your parents have to promise to stick to it, too. It's that magic word, *compromise*, again. Your parents want you around for family dinner? Fine, but then you want to be able to go to the football games with Leslie on Friday nights. Make some trades so that you get time with your friends and still see your parents. How can they argue with that?

2. Bring the party to your house.

Most parents would rather have you and your friends making a mess in the basement than hanging out who knows where. Plus, you can probably get some good snacks and maybe a cool stereo system if you turn your house into the party house. You need some entertainment, right? And everyone knows teenagers are always hungry (for Doritos, Diet Coke, and M&M's, that is—make sure you're there to help with the grocery list).

3. Ask if you can bring your best friend along on family outings.

If your parents are going to make you go to a family dinner or visit your aunt Ida (and she's not even your real aunt), ask if you can bring your BFF along. They may or may not give in, but remind them that they want to get to know your friends better, and this is the perfect chance for some real getting-to-know you time. It's worth a shot. Hey, aunt Ida would probably love your BFF—they have the same taste in jewelry!

> This mom thinks friends can make or break your happiness. Her one piece of advice? "Choose your friends wisely." —Marilee, 40

Hippity-Hop—We're Not Talking *Pat the Bunny* Here

When it comes to music, parents get freaked about anything with semi-sexy lyrics and a serious bass line. They still remember when you were listening to "It's a Small World," and the thought of you singing along to lyrics about drive-bys is enough to send them over the edge. But not all hip-hop is about guns and sex. Only they wouldn't know that because trying to get them to listen to your tunes is like waging World War III.

Time Warp

CDs weren't mass-produced until 1982. When your mom and dad were teenagers, they were listening to cassette tapes, vinyl records, and 8-tracks. Have you ever seen an 8-track? Probably not. That's how outdated they are. But vinyl is back in fashion as a retro way to listen to music. That means your parents are vintage!

Don't lose hope yet. You may still have a chance of breaking Mom and Dad into hip-hop (or pop, or country, or whatever you download). Just remember: no fast movements. Your parental music maneuver is all about easing them in.

1. Change half of their car radio stations to yours. DO NOT CHANGE ALL OF THEM. If your dad is anything like mine, and you change all the stations, you'll be able to hear him screaming from the garage. Tell your parent you're going to give them a taste of your style and then change some of the stations. If something with a few four-letter words comes on and you don't think your mom will be down with it, you can casually change the station and mention, "That song sucks." You definitely want to avoid the "Do You Know What He's Singing About?" lecture.

2. Give your parents' music a chance. Are they into classic rock? After listening to a few of their favorite songs, you might find that you have more in common than you thought. Maybe they'll like that new rock group you discovered on iTunes. Plus, music makes for

perfect, painless get-to-know-you conversation when you're riding around with Mom and Dad.

3. Offer to make your mom a mix of your favorite music. That way you can carefully select songs without a ton of swearing or sexy panting. Your mom or dad might actually like the tunes, and opening up to them in this way will definitely get you somewhere later on — like when you want to go to that rap concert. And you want to take the car. And you need some money for the ticket.

My 10 Favorite Parent-Friendly Albums That Are Still Cool Enough for You
(They don't suck. Promise.)

1. The Rolling Stones, *Let It Bleed.* There's a reason the Rolling Stones are cool again, even though Mick Jagger is old enough to be your grandfather.
2. Wyclef Jean, *The Carnival.* This album is a kind of "easy listening" version of today's hip-hop.
3. Carly Simon, *Greatest Hits.* Who can't sing along to "You're So Vain"?
4. *The Forrest Gump Soundtrack.* It's filled with the good oldies that revolutionized your parents' generation and still rock enough for you.
5. Carlos Santana, *Supernatural.* Everyone can appreciate Santana's sweet guitar skills.
6. Anything by the Ramones. The Ramones played kick-ass punk rock that still kicks ass.
7. Fleetwood Mac, *The Dance.* Stevie Nicks has a serious set of pipes and her version of "Landslide" is still the best.
8. Coldplay, *X&Y.* You might catch your dad listening to this on his own after you introduce him to it.
9. Jimi Hendrix, *Electric Ladyland.* Jimi's best. 'Nuff said.
10. Any and all U2 albums (*Joshua Tree* is my personal favorite). This is just generally good music.

It's All About the Volume

Ever heard this?

"Turn that bass down!"

"This music grates on my nerves!"

"You're going to make yourself deaf."

Everything sounds worse to your parents when it's loud. (Another reason you need an iPod.) But if you're rocking without headphones and want to keep them off your case (and away from your stereo), take it down a notch. But just a notch. You don't live in a museum.

Five Hip-Hop and Pop Albums You Won't Have to Turn Down When Your Parents Walk in the Room

- Usher, *Confessions*
- Gwen Stefani, *Love. Angel. Music. Baby.*
- Beyoncé, *Irreplaceable*
- Chris Brown, *Chris Brown*
- Mariah Carey, *The Emancipation of Mimi*

When Your Parents Turn Your Music Against You

Some parents use music as the ultimate form of punishment. As if hearing them complain about how much they hate punk isn't punishment enough. Life sucks when you can't listen to the music you like, and your parents know it. Here are some examples of how they could use your tunes to their advantage:

Whenever Amy gets in trouble, whether it's 'cause she's ten minutes late for curfew or was caught cutting class, her parents take away all her CDs and her iPod. As if getting your albums confiscated isn't enough, the iPod, too? Torture.

It could be even worse.

One night, when Sophie's parents couldn't find their Paul Simon CD, her dad figured Sophie might have been listening to it. I know what you're thinking. "Who is Paul Simon?" And that's just what Sophie would've said, but she wasn't home. Instead of waiting to ask Sophie if she had the album, her dad went downstairs to her room and went through her CD collection. (Hello, invasion of privacy!) But Sophie's dad didn't even consider the fact that he was going through her stuff. All he could think about were the CDs he found with parental warnings for explicit lyrics and music he didn't approve of.

Sophie had a big surprise waiting for her when she got home that night. Stacked on her desk was one pile of her CDs her parents decided she could keep and another pile they were confiscating. Sophie didn't have a choice. There was screaming, there was door slamming, there was even throwing of CDs across the room, but ultimately, Sophie's parents got their way and took about one-third of her CD collection.

It took Sophie months to start trusting her parents again. She felt like they might go through her stuff at any time, even though

there wasn't anything to find. Not to mention that her parents totally missed the point of trust and privacy. It's one thing to find drugs in your kid's room and freak. (OK, that would be a major problem.) It's another to find a CD you don't approve of. Sophie's parents would've been smart to wait for her to get home and talk it out. Listening to music with occasional swear words was the worst thing she was into. If anything, Sophie's parents had it good. And if they would've just talked to her about the CDs instead of totally flipping out, they might have realized that they could trust her. She might have even thrown out the "bad" CDs on her own.

Most parents aren't crazy enough to lose it over some CDs. So next time they yell to turn the music down or ask, "What on earth are you listening to?" be glad they aren't rooting through your room and taking your music. And then give them a break by turning the volume down a little or skipping to the next song. (You can crank the tunes in the car and they'll never know.)

Chapter **Five**

The Essentials of
Declaring Independence—
Hair Dye, Piercings, and Tattoos

Unless your parents are a rare breed of cool, the following probably aren't the best ways to declare your independence.

1. Come home from a friend's house with a new hole in your nose
2. Sit down at the dinner table with a purple Mohawk
3. Get a large snake tattooed on your arm and neck

Between parents, teachers, coaches, and bosses, your life is pretty controlled by other people. In fact, the only thing you really have any control over is your body, and you're ready to pierce, ink, dye, dread, and shave every last inch of it. Every girl needs to express herself, but what if what your idea of self-expression isn't exactly in line with your parents'? How can you declare your independence without causing open war at home?

This is how your parents see it: They know from personal experience that it's a pretty judgmental world out there. Some people, including potential employers, college professors, and your neighbors, might not be able to look past an eyebrow piercing or tattoo to see what a smart, talented person you are. Your parents don't want you to be limited for the rest of your life by a style decision you made as a teenager. And believe it or not, your parents care about how your piercings and tattoos make them look. They don't want the rest of the neighborhood to think they're letting you run out of control. Top all that off with the fact that your parents might not think your style decision is particularly stylish, and you've got a major dilemma.

This is how you see it: You get it that your parents want you to have every opportunity out there; you don't want to be judged because of a little nose ring or back tattoo either. But just because your dad's sense of style doesn't include red-streaked layers and your best friend's mother thinks belly-button rings are inappropriate doesn't mean you agree with them. In fact, you might think an ankle tattoo is hot!

What to do about it: Talk it out. You know your parents are going to flip when you come home with a nose piercing, a shoulder tattoo, and a new blonde dye-job. So this is one of those situations when it's better to ask forgiveness than permission, right? Wrong. Even though you're on your way to parental freedom, your parents are still technically in charge of you. Walk in the front door with bright-blue highlights and you might never see the keys to the family car (or the outdoors for that matter) again. Why put yourself in that situation? Talk to your parents before making any major changes because they will definitely notice. And asking forgiveness at that point will only get you so far.

Dye It Baby, One More Time

If you're desperate to declare your independence but don't want anything permanent, hair dye is the way to go. You can get a new look without needles (ewww!) or any of the major health risks associated with piercings and tattoos. Also majorly important, if your dye-job goes really wrong (imagine Britney Spears with Kermit the frog–colored curls), you can fix it without going to the emergency room. You'll just need a good stylist!

Chances are, your parents probably won't have a giant problem with you dying your hair. In fact, your mom probably dyes her hair and so, probably, do most of her friends. (Although covering up gray isn't exactly what you're going for.) Just be careful not to do too much coloring—your locks will look as rough as your straw handbag.

Try This at Home vs. Don't Try This at Home

Darker color	Bleach
Lowlights	Highlights
Lemon juice in the sun	Anything green (swimming pool–chlorine dye-job, anyone?)

Hint: Anything with bleach is harder to fix and wreaks havoc on your hair. And even though the do-it-yourself approach to hair care is cheap, it definitely has its risks. Rip a few pictures out of a magazine and take them to a pro to get the look you really want.

Mom Won't Let You Dye Your Hair?

Ask if you can join her at the salon next time she goes. If she's there, nothing can get out of control, right? And you'll get to spend some of that quality time together that she's always talking about. (Hey, maybe she'll even pay for your new do!)

If your parents are sketched out that you want to dye your hair, make it a slow change. Instead of going for bright red at the start, just add a few red highlights or streaks. Ease them into it. Once they see that you don't look like an '80s punk rocker, they should chill out a little.

Hole-y Cow

When your parents were growing up, the only time they saw someone with facial piercings was in *National Geographic* pictures of Aboriginal tribesmen. OK, so maybe that's a stretch, but being pierced is a lot more common these days than it was back then. It's no longer weird to see a professional woman on Wall Street with a delicate nose stud. (Believe me. I know a gorgeous stockbroker who just got a small diamond in her nose.) But since you aren't on Wall Street yet, how can you make your mom and dad see that getting another piercing is just a way for you to express your style? And like it or not, you need to convince them: a lot of piercing places require parental consent if you're under 18.

Before approaching your parents with the big piercing question, do your research. You need to show them your piercing quest isn't a passing phase and that you've thought past what color earrings you want and how your double-piercings will look with your sunglasses. (Doing research will also help you figure out how you really feel before doing anything drastic. Phew!)

Why Your Parents Are Worried (Risks You Need to Know About)

Before you let someone touch your body with a needle, you should be aware of all the risks and know how to keep yourself safe. So, study up before letting anyone with a needle near you.

Check out the Association of Professional Piercers Web site for honest advice on what to look for in a good piercer and what the associated health risks are. **www.safepiercing.org**

The Mayo Clinic Web site also has some good tips on how to protect yourself when you get a new piercing. **www.mayoclinic. com/health/tattoos-and-piercings**

And, of course, you can always ask your family dentist or doctor. Your dentist will be able to tell you what damage a tongue piercing will do to those pearly whites and the doctor will have some general hygiene advice. Take it. They didn't go to school for eight million years for nothing.

No matter what, be sure to get any piercing done professionally. Taking the do-it-yourself approach, with a needle and rubbing alcohol, is just asking for a big nasty scar that will leave your belly button looking totally deformed for the rest of your life. Ask around to find piercing parlors that your friends have had good experiences with and check for yourself to make sure their health standards are first-rate.

If you do get a piercing—no matter where it is—you have to be really careful to let it heal before you start fiddling with new rings. That's just one major reason to consult your parents before you start punching holes in yourself. You don't want to spring an eyebrow ring on your parents, be forced to take it out, and risk getting an ugly scar-tissue lump that makes you look like Quasimodo.

DIY Gone Awry

It was the summer before her junior year of high school, and Annie was enjoying a night out with the girls—gossiping, pizza, chick flicks. Standard GNO stuff. That is, until Liz got the idea that all the girls should pierce their belly buttons. Before anyone really thought about it, they were talking about how Stacie, a senior from school, looked so cute in a bikini with her pierced belly button.

Liz dug around in the linen closet and found a few of her mom's old sewing needles. She emptied all the ice out of the freezer and grabbed a few paper towels. And then it started. After trying to numb their stomachs, they poked the needles through their skin, trying to act like it didn't hurt that badly and trying not to scream from the blood. Finally, after they had the needle all the way through the skin, Liz gave them some fishing wire to keep the holes from closing up until they could get some cool belly button rings.

A few days later, Annie's belly button had turned a nasty purple color and hurt so badly she couldn't sleep on her stomach. She took the ring out, but it was too late. Even a few years later, she still had a gnarly scar. So much for sexy bikini belly!

If you are allowed to get a piercing, visit the body piercing section on **www.WebMD.com** and talk to your piercer to learn more about taking care of your piercing and good piercing hygiene. (Hint: It takes more than a bar of soap.)

If your parents won't give in to reason or begging, try to work it with a little bribery. Your mom really wants you to ace the next math test? Tell her you'll trade a good grade for a trip to the salon to get a cute cubic navel stud. It's worth a shot.

If all else fails, you might be stuck waiting until after graduation to get that third hole in your ear. But that might not be the worst thing. You could change your mind by the time you hit college, and then you won't have to worry about concealer for the bump where your nose ring was. (And you won't have to listen to your parents saying, "I told you so.")

Tattoo Trauma

If you thought it was hard talking to your parents about piercings, you ain't seen nothin' yet. Unless your parents have their own tattoo relic from their rebellious youths, *tattoo* is probably one of the worst words you could say in front of them.

But why exactly do tattoos freak parents out so much? Is it the actual ink or what they think a tattoo might say about you? Why do they, and other people (your history teacher, Uncle Fred, etc.), think tattoos are so awful?

Chances are, it's not the actual tattoo that terrifies your parents, but the permanence of it. They don't want you to regret something you did in your teens when you're 30. And, honestly, the basic idea of tattoos probably freaks them out a little. Some parents still associate tattoos with high-school dropouts and convicts. (It's a throwback to their childhood when a lot of tattooed people were also Hell's Angels.)

You need to remind your parents that "beauty really is in the eye of the beholder." They might think tattoos are distasteful, but you see them as an artful way to express yourself. You've got to prove to your parents that you have a good reason for wanting a tattoo and that you've really thought about it.

Getting a tattoo *is* a major decision. Think of it this way: Are you ready to decide whom you're going to marry? Probably not. Then how can you decide what you want stamped on your ankle for the rest of your life? They're both lifelong commitments, which is why in most states you can't get married or get a tattoo before you're 18 years old. You don't want to rush into marriage, and be sure not to rush into getting a tattoo.

Take movie star Angelina Jolie. She has a few tattoos and even got her second husband's name—Billy Bob—tattooed on her bicep. A pretty committed relationship, right? That was until they got divorced and Billy Bob was suddenly out of the picture. Angelina had to get the tattoo removed. (And it wasn't easy, or cheap.) Do you even know a guy who's worth all that? (The lesson here? In addition to being sure you're ready for a tattoo, NEVER, EVER tattoo a boyfriend's name on your body. Take it from Angelina. It can't end well.)

Just the Facts

• Tattoos are legally banned in Oklahoma.

• In Connecticut, all dogs with tattoos must be reported to the police! (Why would Fido need a tat?)

Take the Tattoo Test

Want to see what a tattoo will be like without actually committing to the ink? Get a temporary or henna tattoo. You'll be able to test the waters and, if you hate the look, you'll know before doing anything permanent. If you got a real tattoo and decided to have it removed, you'd have to deal with the pain and huge expense of laser removal. And even then, it's hard to remove all the ink, so you'd probably still have a spot—kind of like a bleach spot on your favorite jeans, only you can't get new skin. With henna and temporary tattoos, you can play around with designs and mix up your style a little—no strings attached!

If after thinking about the risks, you still really want a tattoo and have a cool idea for one, then think about it for a year or two. Hey, you'll have it your whole life. A year isn't that long. (Actually, it's almost as long as Angelina and Billy Bob were married!) And if you wait for a few years to make your decision, you won't have to worry about your parents anyway!

A Tattoo "Fairy" Tale Gone Wrong

Tara was in college when she decided to get a fairy tattooed on her back. It was supposed to be a feminine fairy with wispy wings and tiny details. She gave the tattoo artist a very specific drawing, and they talked it out before he started his work. So you can imagine Tara's total horror when her delicate fairy ended up looking like the Incredible Hulk. The tattoo wasn't even close to what she wanted! Tara had to wait months for the first disaster to heal before she could get it fixed, and even after the second inking, the fairy still resembles Spiderman's archenemy, the Green Goblin.

The Nine Lamest Tattoos in History
(That I could think of. Feel free to add your own to this list.)

1. *Dude, Where's My Car?* In the movie, the main characters get "Sweet" and "Dude" tattoos on their backs. Dude, not so sweet . . .

2. *Jackass* (more like dumbass) star Steve-O has a huge self-portrait on his back. The tattoo head is actually bigger than his real head. So cocky. So stupid.

3. Actress Brooke Shields has the dog from the Mutts cartoon tattooed just below her belly button. A dog on your stomach? Couldn't anyone talk Brooke out of that one?

4. Actress Melanie Griffith has a yellow pear tattooed on her butt. If there's one place you shouldn't have fruit, it's near your booty.

5. Former *Baywatch* babe Pamela Anderson has "Mommy" tattooed on her finger. She had to change it to "Mommy" from "Tommy" after she and Tommy Lee broke up. Can you see your mom with a "Mommy" tattoo?

6. Butterflies. Sure, they're cute in theory, but can you get any more generic?

7. Soccer star, and total hottie, David Beckham has a tattoo of his wife's name in Hindi. The only problem is that he misspelled "Victoria." So his tattoo says "Vhictoria." How romantic!

8. Rapper (well, sort of) Vanilla Ice has a pumpkin tattoo. He must have thought that would be cute. Or something.

9. This guy James my friend Kathy dated had "Taz," the Tasmanian devil, tattooed on his hip. 'Nuff said.

Chapter SIX

When the Clock Strikes—Curfew

Your parents have watched *Cinderella* one too many times. It's like they think you're going to turn into a pumpkin if you're ten seconds late for curfew. And they want you home before midnight!

Why Parents Love Curfews

- They can't sleep until you're tucked into your bed. So the earlier you're home, the more shut-eye they get.
- They want you to wake up early on Saturday morning to clean your room (and walk the dog and vacuum the living room and mow the lawn).
- The devil comes out at midnight. OK, I'm only joking, but one of my friend's moms used to say this and we were always on the lookout for some guy with horns in red leather carrying a pitchfork. We never saw him.

Your parents are genuinely worried about your safety. Statistically, more crimes and accidents happen at night, and your parents can't stand the thought of something bad happening to you. And hey, deep down you love them for it. You just wish they'd worry until 1:00 AM instead of midnight.

In the land of Teenville, not all curfews are created equal.

Just the Facts

According to *USA Today*, more than 700 cities have teen curfews, meaning the government tells you how late you can be at the mall, at restaurants, and out with friends. At least all your friends have to be in at the same time!

Doesn't it seem like everyone has a later curfew than you? And understandably, when you're the only one who has to be home early, you're bound to be a little late every once in a while. But don't start mumbling excuses yet. Five minutes past midnight doesn't deserve the same excuse as when you waltz in at 2:00 AM. So how late is late?

Parents Talk Back

"The curfew's not a trust issue, it's really a sleep issue. I don't like losing sleep." —Feeny, 56

The 3 Degrees of Lateness

Ten minutes past curfew: Not too bad. Ten minutes is less than the combined length of commercials on during your favorite TV show. If you realize you're going to be late but can get home within ten minutes of curfew, then just get your butt in the car and drive! Calling from the scene isn't worth it at that point. Instead, pull out the cell phone and remind your parents why they're paying $40 a month—so you can call them from the road! You might still be on the phone with your mom when you pull in the driveway, but at least you can say those magic words, "I'm home!" before you walk through the door. If you aren't on the cell when you get home, tell the parents you were definitely trying to make curfew and you'll leave the party a few minutes earlier next time.

Thirty to forty-five minutes past curfew: OK, so you're obviously late but not so late that you're parents are totally fuming—at least not yet. The trick is to call first so they aren't getting progressively more worried (and angry) with every minute you aren't home. Then, when you get home, apologize (sincerely). Tell your parents you're sorry to keep them awake and ask if you can talk about everything in the morning. It's a nice gesture to let them get some sleep, and then you can deal with everything when you're all well rested.

One hour (or more!) past curfew: Two words—you're screwed. Start apologizing as soon as you walk through the door. Chances are you're going to get grounded no matter what you say, but the more remorseful you are, the less time you'll have to stand there while your parents yell at you.

Of course, the best way to avoid being late for curfew is not to be late at all (bet you've heard that before!). If you know your curfew is approaching, and you want to stay out later, call and ask your parents for some extra time instead of just showing up two hours late. Try the "I'm Just Finishing a Movie" tactic. Tell them you're in the middle of a major thriller, and give them a general idea of how much longer you'll be. Chances are they'll appreciate the call and give you an extension. (Just don't use this every weekend. Your parents won't fall for it.)

The Five WORST Excuses for Missing Curfew

1. The guy in front of me was driving sooooo slow. (Your mom will ask if you planned on speeding home.)
2. I fell asleep. (This immediately makes your parents think of sleeping next to someone, which implies sex, which will invite a four-hour discussion about sexual morality.)
3. I forgot what time I had to be home. (This opens up a chance for your parents to create ways to remind you what time you need to be home every night, i.e. grounding you until you can remember.)
4. Lisa doesn't have to be home until 1:00. (Your parents don't care. Really.)
5. I ran out of gas. (Your parents will say that you need to be better prepared and then give you a lecture on maturity.)

These excuses are down for the count, so you've got to have something else up your sleeve that's actually going to work. But be warned, the following excuses work best if you aren't more than 30 minutes late. After that, start begging for mercy (or check out the time-specific excuses earlier in the chapter).

What to Say When You Get Home Late (Weekend Edition)

1. "The party was so much fun, I didn't realize it was so late. I'll leave early next time!"

2. Use your natural charm and say, "I wanted to show up fashionably late." (Hey, maybe they'll think you could be the next stand-up comedy star and go easy on you.)

What to Say When You Get Home Late (Weekday Edition)

1. "I lost track of time because I was studying." (The thought of you with your nose in a book will fill your parents' heads with visions of green college campuses with ivy growing on redbrick buildings and a library with stained-glass windows.)

2. "I was filling up the car so I wouldn't be late to school in the morning." (Hint: You should really have a car to use this one. Otherwise, it's clear you're just full of it.)

"One night my parents called me at 12:01, just one minute past my curfew, and told me I was late. I was just pulling into the driveway, but according to them, I was late if I wasn't physically in the house. Being on the property didn't count!"   —Marie, 16

Time Warp Timeline

The older your parents get, the earlier they want to go to bed (meaning, the earlier they want you home). To figure out what time they consider reasonable for a curfew, check the generational curfew timeline. It reveals what time your parents had to be home when they were teenagers!

The '50s	The '60s	The '70s	The '80s
A really late night for them was 10:00 p.m.!	Most parents wanted their kids home before 10:00 so they didn't turn into hippies!	11:00 to midnight started to become acceptable.	Midnight became standard. (Thank goodness for the '80s!)

You Want Me Home When?!?
(How to Get Later Curfews for Big-Time Occasions)

Even though the average curfew for teenagers is midnight, sometimes 12:00 just won't cut it. You have things to do, people to see, places to go. But what occasions deserve some extra time, and how do you convince your parents to forget the clock so you can stay out past the witching hour?

Prom: This one's a no-brainer. Prom night is bigger than graduation—well, almost. You get all dressed up, ride around in a limo, and have a killer after-party. No way can you make it home by midnight!

Your Birthday: It only comes once a year, and it's an entire day (and night) dedicated to you! If your parents really want to give you a birthday present, they can forget the curfew rules for 24 hours.

Opening Night for a Hot Movie: Sometimes a midnight movie is the only way to be the first to see the latest flick starring your favorite hottie movie star. Your parents can understand a celeb crush, can't they? (Your mom might even want to come along.)

School's Out: The start of summer (and end of school) deserves major celebration. Three months without teachers, homework, and tests! Tell your parents they're going to have you around all summer, a few extra hours without you home won't kill 'em.

You Just Won the Big Game/Aced the SAT/Were Chosen as Mathlete of the Year: Some achievements deserve a little recognition (and a few extra hours on the town). Hey, it's not like your parents are going to pay you for winning that tennis match, so a later curfew is worth a try.

Just the Facts

According to iVillage.com, 71 percent of teenagers have curfews. That means only 29 percent of teenagers don't have to stress about their parents watching the clock. But think about this: Even though 29 percent of teens are more relaxed than most because they don't have a curfew, chances are most of their friends do. So, they still have to deal with curfew-crazy parents to some degree. It's the inescapable law of curfews—they can ruin anyone's night!

Everyone Gets to Stay Out Later Than You

You beg. You cry. You scream. And no matter what, your parents won't change your curfew. They don't care that Abbie doesn't have to be home until 12:30 and Lauren can stay out until 1:00. And you haven't even brought up the fact that Katie doesn't have a curfew at all.

When in Rome, Do As the Romans Do

One way to occasionally get a later curfew is to sleep over at a friend's house. No one's going to blame you for keeping Josie's curfew if you're crashing with her. You're just respecting her house rules. After all, your parents raised you to be a very respectful young adult. It's not like you're trying to cause trouble by staying out an extra hour, you just want to finish the movie with everyone else. One tip, don't try to sleep over at the same friend's house too often; your parents will think something's fishy and eventually catch on to your curfew scam. And definitely don't be late for your friend's curfew. That's just asking for trouble.

If your parents deep-six a sleepover with your BFF, then you have to take drastic action: forget your curfew woes and bring the party to your place. Sure you have to deal with having your parents around, but they can't complain if you're right there in front of them. And being at home means you won't have to leave a party-in-progress to make curfew—it never hurts to have an extra 30 minutes to flirt with your crush, even if it is at your crib!

Chapter **SEVEN**

High-School Hell—Bad
Grades and Other
Scholastic Scrapes

Remember when going to school meant playing kickball at recess and learning to play "Mary Had a Little Lamb" on the recorder during music class? Those were the good old days. If only high school were like elementary school, you'd get gold stars for keeping your locker clean and an A in physics just for giving your teacher an apple.

Oh, how times have changed. Between all your homework and freaking out about the SATs—not to mention prom, keeping up with the latest hallway gossip, and looking cute for your crush—high school is stressful enough without your parents constantly hounding you to try harder and study more. Seriously. Since when is a B a bad grade? Could your parents pass your geometry class? Maybe if they got off your case, you'd actually have time to do your homework.

On the other hand, your parents mean well. While things are a bit different since they were in school (Hello, health class!), your parents do know how competitive it is out there in the real world. All they really want is for you to do well now so you can live well later (and get the heck out of their house). So cut them a little slack. Tell them about the crazy amount of pressure you're under, and assure them that you're trying. Then hand them a quadratic equation to solve.

Surviving Parent-Teacher Conferences

It's unavoidable. No matter how much you dread parent-teacher conferences, they just won't go away. They're like a bad rash and, unfortunately for you, your parents probably won't miss a chance to get the real scoop on your grades and performance.

Aside from crossing your fingers that your parents don't know about the conferences (hey, you aren't going to remind them), there's not much hope for you. The rash has to be treated.

One word of advice: If you are trying to keep your parents from going to parent-teacher conferences, don't come out and say that they don't need to go. And even more importantly, don't tell them which teachers they don't need to see. You might as well paint bull's-eyes on those teachers. You can be sure not only that your parents will go to that parent–teacher conference, but that those teachers are the first ones they'll visit.

You're probably a really good student. But if for some reason you're worried that your teachers and parents are going to conspire against you, ask if you can come along. Tell your parents you want to be more involved in school, and you'd like to hear what your teachers have to say. Your teachers probably won't be as harsh with you sitting right there, and both your parents and teachers will be impressed by how much you care. Plus, you'll probably learn a few things. Teachers often give parents advice about helping their teens study and prepare for next semester. Who knows? Going to parent-teacher conferences might be the answer to getting a good grade on the final.

Just the Facts

For their January 2006 issue, *ELLEgirl* magazine asked 2,000 teenagers to name their biggest causes of stress. Thirty-three percent of them said school and grades. No wonder you get pissed when your parents start in on you to study—you're already worrying about it!

The Top Twelve Funniest High-School Movies of All Time

1. *Mean Girls*
2. *American Pie*
3. *Napoleon Dynamite*
4. *The Breakfast Club*
5. *Clueless*
6. *Fast Times at Ridgemont High*
7. *10 Things I Hate about You*
8. *Grease*
9. *Pretty in Pink*
10. *Sixteen Candles*
11. *Freaky Friday* (the Lindsay Lohan version, of course)
12. And last, but not least, *Ferris Bueller's Day Off*

Homework Sucks

Let's face it: sitting on your bed doing homework is never going to be as fun as chillin' with your friends. But unless you're a child genius, you're stuck with it. So, why not make homework work for you?

Four Ways to Make Homework Less Work

1. Start a study group.

Your parents can't complain that you're spending too much time with your friends if you're doing your homework. And it might even be a good excuse to spend some time with your crush!

2. When it's time to do chores, pull out the books.

Sitting at the kitchen table doing homework is a great way to get out of emptying the dishwasher and even cleaning your room. Yeah, you'll probably have to help out sooner or later, but why not make it later and get your homework done in the meantime?

3. Get more computer time.

Your parents can't complain that you're IM'ing too much if you're asking your BFF about your math homework. (You can get some good gossip in between problems, too!)

4. Get your props.

Are your parents giving you grief about studying more? Have them give your math homework a shot. They'll probably be totally lost and have more respect for what you're learning.

Senioritis: \'sē-nyər-ĭ-təs\ (noun)
Also known as senior slack and senior slump, *senioritis* is a serious condition that often occurs after college acceptance letters have arrived during a student's senior year. Symptoms include procrastination, staring longingly out classroom windows, and increased social activity. Although senioritis is not recognized by the American Medical Association, studies show it is exacerbated by warm weather and boring classes. The only known cure is summer vacation.

So how much of that homework are you actually going to use in the real world? Here's a hint: not much. But there are a few classes you really should stay awake for.

English: Whether you're writing your college application essay or writing an e-mail, knowing how to write well is super important.

Just the Facts

Your parents may not want you to sign up for weight lifting when you could be taking AP chemistry, but who's to say there isn't value in learning something different? According to *Seventeen* magazine, "79 percent of high school seniors say they aren't very interested in school." So, if weight lifting adds some spice to your schedule and makes it easier to handle your other demanding classes, why shouldn't it be part of your day? As long as you're taking the required courses, you deserve to have some fun with your electives.

Geometry: Believe it or not, understanding right angles will help when you're trying to hang that Jay-Z poster in your dorm room and will come in handy when you're trying to sink the eight ball in your next game of pool.

P.E.: Getting exercise never gets old. Plus, you never know when you're going to meet some really hot guy at the gym.

Any foreign language: Hello, study abroad and cute foreign-exchange students!

Report Cards: Why You Should Care

If only getting a C meant you were cool. Social skills are an important part of life, right? Just try telling that to your dad when he sees your report card at the end of the year and realizes you aren't going to Harvard because you spent all year texting your BFF during math class.

But your dad has a point. When you fail a class, you risk losing your shot at the future you want so badly. College is your chance to get out on your own, and you definitely don't want to screw it up just because you hate chemistry homework or think the guy sitting in front of you has a nice smile.

After graduation, your grades are yours. They are going to shape your future, not your parents'. So next time your mom starts harassing you to study more, remember that it's because she wants you to succeed.

"What the F-minus?" —Principal Skinner on *The Simpsons*

Surviving the Report-Card Storm

There's nothing more frustrating than bombing a test you totally studied for. That is, nothing except having the bad grade e-mailed to your parents within minutes of seeing it yourself.

Thanks to new technology, a lot of schools are e-mailing parents with report cards, attendance, and even individual test scores on a weekly, and sometimes daily, basis.

It would be one thing if your parents got an e-mail with your report card at midterms and then at finals. That's when report cards are sent out any-way, and you can deal with having the report card conversation two times a semester. But a weekly update? Not even Super Teen can handle a talking-to about grades every single week.

SUBJECT	GRADE
MATH	A-
SCIENCE	B-
US HISTORY	C+
ENGLISH	B
DRIVERS ED.	A+

Talk about micromanaging. How are you supposed to learn any sort of responsibility or even have a normal conversation with your parents when they know more about your school performance than you do?

Since you aren't going to change school policy, and you don't even want to try hacking into the system to change your dad's e-mail address (you think you have problems now?), your only hope is a heart-to-heart with your parents.

Be honest with your mom and dad about how much stress the daily e-mails are adding to your life. You have enough pressure to do well in school without having to come home and talk about grades, tests, and college every single night. Suggest that your parents get the e-mails once a month or every two weeks. That's manageable and probably less than you talk about grades and report cards with them already. If your grades are decent and you aren't a total hellion, your parents probably won't have a problem with cutting back. Who knows? They might find the weekly e-mails kind of annoying. They probably dread the daily grade confrontation as much as you do.

Three of the Worst Students in History and Why They Would Make Your Parents Proud

1. Albert Einstein

Did you know he barely passed math class? And now he's considered the most important scientist of the twentieth century. More proof that grades aren't everything!

2. Steve Jobs

The founder of Apple might be a computer genius, but that doesn't mean he was brilliant in school. He actually dropped out of college after six months, but he didn't stop studying things that interested him, like calligraphy. Then he took everything he learned and created the first Mac computer. Why do you think Macs have such great fonts?

3. Pablo Picasso

One of the greatest artists in history, and the cofounder of Cubism, Picasso was a terrible student, even when he was five. But that didn't stop him from being passionate about art and using his talents to redefine art in the twentieth century. The point? Passion and hard work matter more than grades.

When Good Grades Aren't Good Enough for Mom and Dad

Picture this: It's report card day and you got a C in AP biology. You've never had to work so hard and that C might as well be a Purple Heart. You get home, pull the report card out of your bag, and leave it on the kitchen counter for your parents to see. Hey, you're proud that you managed an average grade in a college-level class. And for good reason!

Dinner comes around, and when you sit down at the table, your parents start talking about your report card. But instead of toasting the fact that you managed to do better than 70 percent of the rest of the class, your parents pull out those five little words: "We expect more from you." They aren't happy that a C is bringing down your GPA. They might as well slap you in the face.

It would be one thing if you brought home a big fat F, but a C? It's hard not to be totally crushed when it seems like your best isn't good enough for your parents.

But before you storm away from the table, be sure your parents know your side of the story. Do they realize how hard this class was for you? Have you told them how happy you are with the C and how hard you worked the entire semester?

Once your parents see that this isn't any normal C—because you really did your best—they'll probably apologize and be more realistic with their expectations. Most parents just want their teens to work hard; your parents are probably the same. They don't expect more than your best effort.

But if your parents are total perfectionists, you may not get the apology or credit you deserve. No matter what, don't feel inadequate. You know how hard you've worked. Don't let anyone convince you that your best isn't good enough—even when your best isn't perfect.

Skipping/Ditching/Cutting/Sluffing

It's all the same no matter how you say it: skipping class is skipping class and, as much as your parents scream and yell about it, it's a part of high school. You know they did it. We're not talking about cutting all your classes every day, just an occasional Ferris Bueller–style ditching session in order to stay sane for the rest of the year.

The most important thing for successful school skipping is to save your ditch days for when you really need them. Don't miss essential grade days, like tests or presentations. It will be totally obvious why you're gone, and you'll be in deep at report-card time. And don't do anything stupid while you're out and about. If you think you'll get in trouble for ditching class, just wait and see how deep you are when you get caught breaking a house rule or, worse, a law, when you're skipping school. Also, be sure to spread out your skipping efforts among all your classes so one teacher doesn't get suspicious. You don't want to miss any one class more than two times or you'll be really screwed for finals. Extra credit only goes so far.

Since skipping school means risking getting caught, you've got to be prepared when someone sees you leaving campus, car keys in hand. You'd better believe that your parents don't approve of these oh-so-necessary missed classes, so it's important to be ready for that dreaded call from the attendance office: "Mr. Smith, Leslie was caught skipping class today."

Play the "I Needed a Break" card.

You can't convince your parents that skipping school is OK if you're failing all your classes. But if you're getting good grades and rarely miss a day, you can use this to your advantage. Tell your parents how prepared you are for upcoming tests and projects and remind them how few times you've been absent in the past. They've probably called in sick to work before and gone to see a movie. Assure them you've got your homework under control and you might be able to get off with a warning.

Know when to surrender.

If you want to get out of the skipping-school confrontation alive, you have to recognize when you're beat. Technically, you've already been caught, so your parents know you're guilty. Lying and making up excuses will just get you in deeper. Admitting you skipped, and accepting the consequences, is a major sign of maturity.

Going Mental

We all reach a point sometimes when we just can't face the day. We're exhausted from the busy-ness of life and need a little "mental health" recuperation. Once or twice a year, my mom used to let me take a day off from school. (Of course, I had to be caught up on my homework and promise I didn't have any major tests or assignments coming up.) I spent the day hanging out—talking with my mom, reading, watching bad daytime TV, and basically relaxing. Of course, if I was caught skipping class, the mental health days were out. I was always better off telling my mom when I needed a break rather than taking matters into my own hands. And even better, these mental health days were excused by my mom, so I didn't have to worry about unexcused absences on my attendance record!

The Not-So-Excused Absence

When I was a sophomore, my best friend, Jill, and I were inseparable. If we weren't hanging out together then we were on the phone or on our way to meet somewhere. So when Jill's parents went out of town and she needed someone to sleep over, it was only natural that I should be the one to keep her company. My parents were cool with me staying over as long as I didn't miss ANY classes.

I swore up and down that I would be at school on time, and I really didn't have any plans not to be. That was, until Jill and I stayed up most of the night watching movies and talking about our latest crushes. The next morning I was zonked and when the alarm went off, I barely even opened my eyes before hitting the "off" button.

I slept like a baby until about noon, when I realized I'd missed most of the day and my parents were going to be getting a call from the principal. I knew if my parents found out that I'd skipped class, they wouldn't let me stay with Jill the rest of the week.

So being the clever teenagers we were, Jill and I came up with a plan. Jill called the attendance office pretending to be my mother so I could get an excused absence. It was working like a charm until the secretary got suspicious and asked Jill for the birthdays of my brother and sisters. She wanted to verify that Jill was really my mother. I knew we were screwed when Jill said, "I just have so many kids. I can't keep all their birthdays straight." The secretary actually laughed out loud and then proceeded to call my mom at home. Within ten minutes, I was grounded for two weeks with no car.

Thanks for nothing, Ferris Bueller!

Chapter **EIGHT**

The Road to Freedom—
Your Driver's License

After 16 years of being at your parents' complete and total mercy, the day finally comes when you can drive off into the sunset. You're 16, and the world is your highway. Well, sort of. You may have a driver's license, and if you're lucky a sweet ride, but that doesn't mean your parents are out of the picture. In fact, they might be hounding you more than ever.

"Don't drive so fast."

"Take your little sister to piano lessons."

"If you talk back again, I'm going to take the car away."

Sound familiar? On the road of life there are many teenagers, and behind every teenager is a nagging parent.

Driving Miss Crazy

The first time I ever drove with my mom, she held on to the door handle with such a death grip, I practically had to peel her fingers off the plastic when we finally pulled into the mall parking lot.

That would have been bad enough, but on the drive, every time a car changed lanes in front of me or I checked my blind spot, my mom gasped like it was her last breath. She was freaking me out so much that, if I was as bad of a driver as she made it seem, we would have died within five minutes of pulling out of the driveway.

Parents are the ultimate backseat drivers, even if they're in the front. They get so freaked out when you are in the driver's seat that you can't even concentrate on the lanes because you're worried they're going to hyperventilate in the passenger seat. But do they ever watch how they drive? If your parents are anything like mine, your dad can't go two miles without making someone carsick and your mom sometimes talks to the other cars on the road like they can hear her. They definitely don't inspire confidence. And they're your role models for good drivers? They're just lucky you paid attention in driver's ed.

Before You Get the Keys

In most states—35 to be exact—you need a learner's permit before you can get your driver's license. Not a big deal, except that your parents have to give permission for you to apply for a learner's permit even if you're enrolled in driver's ed.

Most parents aren't so ridiculous that they won't let you get your permit, but if yours are totally against it and won't sign your permission form, you're in for some serious negotiating. Here's where Chapter 2 comes in; take a little refresher course before negotiating with mom and dad for the keys. And don't forget to remind them that once you have your license, you will be able to

Just the Facts

In most states, you have to wait to get your license until you're 16, but in some you have to be even older. And in others, you can get behind the wheel when you're as young as 14.

run a few errands for them or drive yourself to basketball practice. Hey, you don't mind picking your little brother up from soccer as long as you get some time behind the wheel. (And who says you can't stop at your BFF's house for a few minutes on the way?)

Your State Says You Have to Be How Old to Drive?

Connecticut: 16$^1/_2$ years

Idaho: 15 years (but you can only drive in daylight)

Indiana: 16 years, 1 month, and 1 day

Maryland: 17 years and 7 months

Massachusetts: 16$^1/_2$ years

Montana: 15 years

New Jersey: 17 years (with some restrictions)

New York: You have to be at least 18 to drive in Manhattan, but 16 works for the rest of the state

South Carolina: 15 years

South Dakota: 14 years

Virginia: 16 years and 3 months

Check out **www.dmv.org** to get the whole 411 on your state's driver's license laws.

When They Hold the Car Over Your Head

Since your parents probably know how badly you want to drive, and they have the power to make it possible (if you're not 18, they have to give you the go-ahead and the car keys), they can use your driver's license as a bribe. Here are a few horror stories.

• Jeff's parents wouldn't let him get his license until he got his Eagle Scout award. What exactly does knot-tying have to do with vehicle safety? Nothing, but at least he could prove he was responsible before he finally got behind the wheel.

• Melissa's parents told her she couldn't drive unless she got a 3.8 GPA or higher. Let's be honest, you're going to have more time to study for those 3.8 grades if you can drive home from school instead of taking the bus.

• Amanda's parents took the car away when she wouldn't stop dating a guy they didn't like. It's not like Amanda couldn't see her man at school. And he had a car. Didn't her parents think about the fact that when Amanda was the one driving, at least her parents knew about their dates? Taking the car away didn't solve anything for them, and Amanda got into more trouble when she was caught cruising around with the guy.

Some parents think taking the car away is worse than grounding you for the weekend or stopping your allowance for a week. In their minds, it's a simple equation:

Teenager – Car = At Their Mercy

And unfortunately, the equation is pretty accurate. But what your parents don't realize is that, when you're without a car, they'll be stuck driving you around. The trick to getting your parents to give back the keys is to turn your punishment into their punishment. Here's how: When your mom or dad asks you to run to the store to buy milk for dinner or to pick up your little brother from his friend's house, remind them that you are banned from the road. They'll tell you that your punishment is only in place when they want it to be (so you'll probably end up running the errand anyway), but you should definitely tell them you don't like double standards. In your least know-it-all voice, let your parents know they can't just pick and choose when you can and can't drive. If they want you to drive to the store for them, you should be able to drive to the movies for yourself.

Just the Facts

According to a *USA Today/ CNN/Gallup* poll from December 2004, most Americans (61 percent to be precise) think that 16-year-olds are too young to drive. And 53 percent think licenses should not be issued until the age of 18. By being a good driver, you can change the bad reputation teens have! Plus you won't have to worry about tickets and accidents.

Of course, if your parents are too smart for this tactic, you're stuck car-less for a little while. That's when friends with wheels come in particularly handy.

Five Ways to Prove You're Responsible with the Car

1. Always wear your seatbelt.

It's not like this is some big show for your parents since you probably wear it anyway (duh, you've seen those after-school specials), but your parents will be happy to see that you're being smart and thinking about your safety. In the words of rapper Kanye West, "Thank God I'm not too cool for the safety belt." (And he should know since he almost died in a car wreck but lived because he had his seat belt on.)

2. If your mom or dad is going to use the car after you, leave it with a full tank.

I know it's hard to part with that $40, but next time you need to borrow a ten-spot (or more!), you can remind your parents about how you left them with plenty of gas.

3. Get the tires rotated.

Most cars need tires to be rotated every 5,000 miles or so. It actually makes the tires last longer and saves your parents cash in the long run. What parent can argue with a teenager who's trying to save them money?

4. Pay your parking tickets on time.

You can't help it if the high-school parking-ticket patrol keeps finding ways to get your money. But since your car is probably registered to your parents, they'll definitely find out if you forget to pay the tickets and the fines start adding up. They'll be pissed, and you will be too when you have to empty your savings account to pay them off.

5. Check the oil.

Don't worry—it's really easy and you don't even have to get your hands dirty. If you don't know how to do this, ask your mom or dad to show you. You can pull the "I'm Trying to Be Responsible" card and get some major props.

Checking the Oil Like a Pro

1. Pop the hood (duh!).

2. Find the oil tank. In most cars, it's located in the front right-hand side of the engine, but ask the gas-station attendant if you can't find yours.

3. Pull the dipstick out of the tank and wipe it off with a paper towel.

4. Once the dipstick is clean, dip it into the oil tank and pull it back out. Look at the oil level. It should come up to one of the level lines on the dipstick (full, empty, etc.)

5. If the tank is full, you're good to go. If not, you can buy a small jug of oil at the gas station or parts store and pour it in yourself.

The Family Car

If you're lucky, your family car is a Jetta or Jeep. But chances are,

Just the Facts

Most insurance companies give a discount to teenagers who are on the honor roll. They think if you're smart enough to get good grades, you're smart enough to handle driving a car. If the insurance company trusts you to be out on the road, shouldn't your parents?

the car you'll get to drive will be a Volvo or Taurus. Parents tend to like "reliable" and "practical" cars. BORRRING! But at least you have some wheels. And just because it's tan and only goes ten miles per hour up hills, doesn't mean you can't ride in style. Before you pull out of the driveway crank up some tunes, put on some lip gloss, and slip on your shades. You definitely won't be mistaken for your mom.

Life in the Fast Lane

Once you start driving, the sound of sirens will make your stomach turn. It feels like cops are lurking around every corner waiting to pull over innocent teenagers. Can they smell fresh meat?

Truth be told, they're waiting to pull anyone over, not just you and your friends. If your dad were at the right place at the right time driving the right (or should we say wrong?) speed, he'd get pulled over as quickly as you would. But that's no consolation when you get a ticket.

As if getting pulled over isn't bad enough, you have to go home and tell your parents about it. Don't you hate having to tell your parents when you've screwed up? But as with most things in life, the reaction they give you depends a lot on your presentation. Here's how to break the news gently.

Cry.

Sometimes crying isn't a bad thing. And if you're like me, you won't be able to help the waterworks, they'll just turn on automatically. By the time you stop crying and tell your parents what happened, they'll be over the initial shock. Just don't overdo it. You don't want your parents to think you're insincere.

Remind your parents about their own past tickets.

After you've calmly told your parents how awful you feel about getting a ticket, ask if they know how you feel. Bringing up their tickets will remind them that they're only human—and so are you. They might even have a good story that will make you laugh or at least feel better.

Offer to go to traffic school.

This way, you can make up for the ticket and get the points taken off your license. Not only does this make you look responsible, it makes you seem like you're thinking long-term, the perfect combination to get your parents thinking you've already learned something from this ticket and don't need additional punishment. Plus, if you work the points off your license, you won't have to worry about having a bad record when you buy your own wheels!

Sibling Rivalry—Chevy Style

As if you don't have enough trouble already, with your older sister wearing your favorite sweater or your little brother stealing your CDs. Throw a car into the mix and you might as well call it sibling warfare. You all want to go out on Friday night, hit the mall with friends on Saturday, and have the car during lunch so you can get off campus. And to add to it, your parents promise to sell the car the next time they hear you fighting over who drove it last. How can you avoid a full-on battle every time you have to go somewhere?

1. Set up a schedule so you get the car at least one weekend night every week. It sucks you can't have it the whole weekend, but at least you'll be good to hit the town once before the Monday grind starts up again. If you get the car Friday, have your BFF pick you up on Saturday. And ask your parents to help with gas money for your friends. You're saving them from listening to fighting about the car, after all.

2. Trade weekdays or weeks so each of you get the car at least a few school days. Unless your sister is the next Olympic gold-medal-winning ice skater and has to get to the rink every morning, you deserve to have the car as much as she does. If you have to bum rides with your friends every once in a while then so does she.

3. Make sure you create a system for gas. It's not fair for you to pay for your older brother's dates and your little sister's Slurpee runs. If your parents aren't going to fill up the car, keep a general pot that everyone contributes to so the car isn't always empty. And tell your sister no stealing from the pot, no matter how much she wants those killer boots.

What's Up with That?

A number of states have laws that keep teenage drivers from using cell phones when they're driving. Like you're any more dangerous than that lawyer who drives around talking on his cell phone, drinking his latte, and checking his BlackBerry. Seriously. But they do have a point. No one should be cruising around if they aren't focusing on the road. And since you haven't had your license as long as Mr. Lawyer, you should definitely put the cell down. (He should too, but that's another issue.)

Don't Pull a Rachel

One day while driving to school, Rachel got pulled over for driving 20 miles per hour over the speed limit. She cried and promised the cop she would slow down. Since Rachel didn't have any tickets on her record (her crying got her out of a lot of close calls), the cop let her go with a warning. A few hours later, during lunch period, Rachel got pulled over again. Same day. Same road. Same cop. Same 20 miles per hour over the speed limit!

It wasn't pretty. The officer didn't feel bad about giving her the full ticket and lectured her for 15 minutes on not learning from her mistakes. This time Rachel was crying for real. She ended up having to go to traffic school to work the ticket off her record. And to make matters worse, her mom wasn't happy to find out that their insurance rates were going up because of Rachel's expensive ticket. Rachel found herself car-less for the next month.

Chapter **NINE**

Work It—After-School Jobs,
Allowances, and Cold, Hard Cash

Life requires a little cash. We're not talking millions here—just enough to fill up the car, see a movie with your friends, and get those rockin' jeans you saw at the mall (and, OK, put a little dough in the college fund your parents started).

But what if your parents don't want you to get a job because they think you should be studying? How can you tell them that your meager $10-a-month allowance isn't going to cut it without sounding greedy and totally pissing them off? Or, what if they want you to get a job and you just aren't ready for that kind of commitment? (Hey, a job takes more time than a boyfriend and definitely gets in the way of a social life.)

Since your parents are putting you up and most likely paying for food and basic life necessities, money can be a sensitive topic. You've got to learn how to talk to them about what you need (and what you want) and figure out some ways you can both leave the table with a few bills in your hands.

It's All about the Benjamins

Rapper and producer P. Diddy, or Diddy, or whatever his name is now, had it right with one of his first chart-topping songs. It is all about the Benjamins—at least for most of life's necessities: gas, car insurance, clothes, shoes, midnight stops at McDonald's (there's no substitute for French fries), prom, and all the other things that have price tags.

For a lot of teenagers, by the time school is over and choir practice is finished, there isn't time for a "real" job. And if you don't have your own wheels and can't get a ride to work, a job might not even be a real possibility. That's when you start counting on the parents for payday (aka an allowance).

You know that old saying, "Money doesn't grow on trees"? Parents like to think that you understand the value of a dollar and aren't expecting them to just hand out bills. But asking for money doesn't mean you necessarily have to do **extra** work—you just need to do a good job of presenting your natural teen wonderfulness.

"I Need an Allowance"

You can't just flat-out ask for cash. Use these arguments to convince your parents to share the wealth:

• An allowance teaches financial responsibility, something you are definitely going to need when you're in college. Work out a deal that you'll learn to budget if you have a weekly or monthly allowance. Once you've learned some financial management, you won't get stuck calling home totally broke during your freshman year.

• School and extracurricular activities take precious time, and there are only 24 hours in a day. Plus, you have 50+ more years to have a job, and by then it's too late to worry about getting into a good college. If your parents really want you to succeed, ask if they'll help make it happen by supporting you. (Financially, that is.)

• According to a study by the National Research Council and the Institute of Medicine, teen students who work more than 20 hours a week don't do as well in school, sleep less, don't get enough exercise, and are more likely to use drugs. Just run that by your parents. The wallet will probably be out before you even finish.

"I Need a Bigger Allowance"

If you already get an allowance, asking for more money can be tricky. You don't want to come off as totally greedy. These tactics can help.

•If you worked overtime at a regular job, you would get paid overtime. Nicely ask your parents to pay up for all the work you do around the house. Hey, that dishwasher doesn't empty itself. You're happy to help out, but you'll be happier with a little financial recognition. Just don't push it too far. You're expected to help out in return for a roof over your head and those Honey Nut Cheerios you eat for breakfast every morning. So only ask for cash for any work you do that's above and beyond the normal call of teen duty.

•You're kicking butt in school, but there's no way you could study enough if you had a job on top of everything else. If your parents want you to keep scoring As, suggest they pitch in to your school success with cash for report cards, test scores, and essay grades. It's money well spent, especially if you end up getting a college scholarship.

Allowance Tip: If you want to keep the cash coming, always thank your mom or dad when they hand over the dough. A little gratitude goes a long way and not just with parents. Thanking your boss for a bonus or a teacher for giving you a break on your homework makes you seem mature and shows you appreciate when someone does something nice for you. And hey, you'll feel good for being grateful.

"While my dad finished college, my mom worked full-time as a teacher for a salary of $6,000 a year. That wouldn't even pay for a car now! No wonder they're so sensitive when I ask for a 10-spot." —Katie, 15

Parents Talk Back

How bad do you really want to ask your mom to buy you that gray sweater? One mom says her biggest fight with her daughter is about "taking care of her clothes and room. It's a source of contention because I don't want to buy her clothes if they are just going to end up dirty on her floor (for months) after the first wearing." —Suzanne, 50

Paper or Plastic?

How many times have you been fumbling around for cash when the person in front of you whips out a credit card and, voilà, walks away in seconds with bags of merchandise? Credit cards can seem like the answer to all financial woes but, unless you're 18, you can't get a credit card without a parent to co-sign. And that might not be a bad thing.

A lot of credit card companies target teens because they want your money. If the credit card company can get you to charge your gas and McDonald's runs and just pay off the minimum balance

each month, they can charge you interest. Essentially, you're paying the credit card company extra cash for lending you the dough to buy that lime green sweater you bought last winter. Did you realize the sweater was costing you more than the price tag? And that might not be the only thing that's costing you more than it's worth. Unless you pay off your card balance every month, credit can be a scary cycle.

The safest way to deal with credit cards is to wait until you've had some experience with a checking account before getting one. That way you'll be able to practice balancing your budget before charging away. But if your parents are all gung ho to get you set up with some plastic, then let them. Just be sure you can pay for everything you charge in cash. You don't want to end up as part of the whopping 80 percent of college students who are in credit card debt before they even graduate. And remember, when in doubt, just pay with bills.

Just the Facts

According to the JumpStart Coalition for Personal Financial Literacy, one out of every three high-school kids has a credit card. That's a lot of credit cards! If one of those is yours, just be sure it doesn't take you straight into debt.

Workin' 9 to 5

It's more like 5 to 9, but you get the idea. If an allowance isn't going to happen, or it's not enough to fund your life, then you're going to need a part-time job. So start writing your resume, and ask your parents if they have any ideas. They might know someone who needs part-time help running office errands or answering phones. If you don't have any hook-ups, boot up the computer. It's time to check the want ads. Here are some good places to start:

Need a job?

Start searching online with these popular employment Web sites:

• www.Monster.com—One of the most popular job sites. Check it out.

• www.GetThatGig.com—Lists summer jobs and internships.

• www.SummerJobs.com—Just what it sounds like, a summer job site.

• www.GrooveJob.com—Great reference site for creating a resume and finding a part-time job.

• www.CareerBuilder.com—Another site that's good for job basics.

For more sites, just go to Google. There are hundreds—and new ones every day.

Remember that where you live might actually affect what kind of job you can get. To get the 411 on your state's teen-labor laws, check out: www.youthrules.dol.gov/states.htm

Creating a Resumé

Notice that this section isn't called Writing a Resumé? That's because a resumé is more than just a list of your skills and talents. It takes a little creativity to say why you're the best person for a job. You've got to sell yourself.

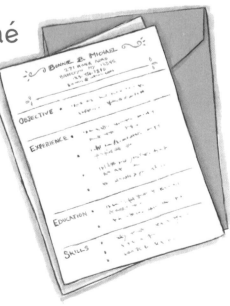

1. Start with your contact information at the top—you want the manager to be able to reach you if she loves your resume!

2. Then list your experience. Include any real on-the-job experience and anything else that might make you an appealing candidate. Do you regularly volunteer at the Boys & Girls Club? Spend time organizing events for your church's youth group? Experience is anything that makes you better qualified to do the job you're applying for. Be creative!

3. Education comes next. No one expects you to have a master's degree when you're 16, but if you've taken any special classes on top of your regular high-school course load, be sure to include those as well. And don't forget to mention if you're on the honor roll or are taking advanced and honors classes. Employers want someone who works hard!

4. After education, highlight any awards or special recognition you've received. Anything and everything from winning the state swimming championship to taking third place in the school spelling bee.

5. And finally, list your personal interests. You're more than just your education and experience, so let that shine through. Employers like well-rounded employees, so if you're a great photographer or like to run, make sure they know it.

After you've had someone proofread your resume, print it out on nice paper (not that generic, white, printer paper) and go get 'em!

Beyond Babysitting
A Few of the Best Part-Time Jobs

Running your own lemonade stand might have been a great way to make money when you were six, but now that you're living in the real world, a 95-cent profit isn't anything to get excited about. You need some real dough. So, aside from paper routes, babysitting, and mowing the lawn, how can you bring home the bacon?

Retail.

Being on your feet is hard work, not to mention the long hours and weekends, but a job at the Gap or Sam Goody will give you fly discounts on clothes and CDs. (Just don't spend your whole paycheck before you get out of the store.) And since these types of stores are often open later than your regular 9-to-5 operations, companies want teenagers who have a little flexibility in their schedules. That's you!

Tutoring.

Use your book-smarts for something other than grades. Offer to tutor kids in your neighborhood, or even your classmates, in exchange for some dough. Chances are, their parents want them to get help, and they'll pay your tutoring fees. Even better? You can set your own hours and don't have to stand on your feet for the entire shift.

Restaurants/Coffee Shops.

The restaurant biz has tons of job possibilities—waiter, dishwasher, host, busboy (or shall we say, busgirl?)—it's just a matter of working your way up and surviving the physical work. At most places, you'll have to work for a while before becoming a waitress, but once you're there, the tips can be killer. In fact, the main reason you want a job in the food industry is because you can get major tip money.

Let's Barter, Baby.

Money isn't everything. Sometimes you can get what you want without paying a penny. Are you dying to borrow your older sister's leather jacket? Offer to trade something she wants to wear, like your favorite vintage bracelet, in return. If bartering worked for centuries in ancient Europe, it can definitely work for you.

Get Creative.

Does everyone love the cute bracelets you make? Do you know how to design Web sites? Use your skills to pay the bills. Nobody ever said the only way to make money is being a slave to corporate America.

And those aren't the only options. Practically everywhere you look, there's a way to make money. Thomas Edison once said genius is "one percent inspiration and ninety-nine percent perspiration," meaning you just have to be willing to work at something to be successful, even if it means walking your neighbor's poodle.

You're Not the Next Tyra Banks

No one's trying to crush your dreams here (or say you're ugly). It's just about being realistic. As nice as it would be to be America's Next Top Model, chances are it's just not going to happen. (And if it did, who knows if you'd really love it?) Don't waste a lot of time figuring out ways to become a professional model, pop singer, or whatever it is Paris Hilton does. You'd be better off playing the lotto. (But not until you're 18, OK?)

Don't Be a Job Snob

No one starts off a career as the editor-in-chief of *Glamour*. Whether you want to be a doctor, a stay-at-home mom, or the next president of the United States, chances are your first job is going to be unglamorous and low on the totem pole. But that doesn't mean it's not worth it. Everyone has to start somewhere. Plenty of successful and famous people started off at the local gas station and worked up from there.

• Singer Macy Gray flipped burgers at McDonald's.
• Actor Robin Williams got his start as a street mime.
• Country singer Clint Black went door-to-door, selling subscriptions for his hometown newspaper, the *Houston Post*.
• Jerry Seinfeld was a lightbulb salesperson while he got his comedy career rolling.
• Mariah Carey had a string of waitressing gigs before she made it big, and she actually got fired from one job as a hat checker.
• Before he was a Hollywood star, Jack Black did cereal commercials to pay rent.
• Actor Jerry O'Connell spent his days mowing lawns and trimming trees as a landscaper for one of his first jobs.
• Danny DeVito, hairdresser? You'd better believe it!
• "Sexiest Man Alive" Brad Pitt has had almost as many weird jobs as he's had movie roles, and one of them was moving refrigerators.
• Best-selling author Steven King was inspired to write his first novel while working as a janitor.

To Work or Not to Work—True Tales from the Teen Workforce

Samantha had a great job at a growing company. The only problem? Her parents. They hated her long hours, the fun-loving atmosphere of the job, and especially the "older guys" she worked with.

"My parents nagged me to get a job to fill some of my free time. They thought I was being unproductive and that I could use a little extra cash. So, naturally, when I scored a job at Abercrombie & Fitch, I was thrilled. Their reaction was not as predictable. Instead of stopping their nagging, it just changed the nature of it. They were skeptical of how I obtained the job and why. Once I started working, they were irritated by the hours, how often I worked, and getting me to work. They even questioned the quality of people I worked with. But I still had the extra cash to look forward to, right? Wrong. Since I now had a job, they felt it unnecessary to pay for my gas, my clothes, and other luxuries I had enjoyed for free pre-job. Getting a job definitely didn't get them off my back as hoped. In fact, I think it just gave them a leg up."
—Samantha, 17

It took Samantha a while to figure out the work/school/parents balance. Her job ended up creating tension with her parents that just wasn't worth it. In the end, she quit and took them up on their offer to help pay for gas. Everyone was much happier. Take it from her and consider all sides of your situation before deciding whether to work or not.

Chapter TEN

Cyber-Life

When your parents were teenagers, phones had rotary dials and were attached to the wall with bolts and cords. And there was only, like, one computer in the world and it was bigger than a Hummer. (No joke!) As for the Internet, it didn't even exist when they were born. Cell phones, texting, instant messaging, blogging, iPods, even e-mail can be like another universe for them.

The worst part is, what your parents don't understand, they definitely don't like. For example:

• They hate it when you text your friends—"Just pick up the phone and call."
• They threaten to take away your cell phone if it rings after 10:00 PM—"I don't care if Lisa's boyfriend just dumped her. You'll see her at school tomorrow."
• They complain that you're wasting your life on the computer—"You're becoming a zombie."

But by opening their eyes to the joys of technology, you can change that, or at least get them to ease up a bit.

Cell Society

Back in the good old days, if your parents were hanging out with friends and needed to make a call, they had to find a pay phone, insert a coin, and stand there while they talked. No wonder they get so mad when you jabber away on your cell.

They nag you about talking too much, texting too much, and your "obnoxious" ringtone. What's up with that? Too much chatting and texting can lead to huge overage charges, and you know how parents feel about bills—the same way you feel about report cards. So, aside from giving up your phone altogether, what's the best way to get your parents off your case?

Five Simple Steps for Getting Your Parents to Stop Complaining About Your Cell

1. Show them how to work their phones. How many parents do you know that have cell phones but can't even open a text message? Your parents will be much more cell-friendly if you teach them some texting basics. Plus, they might get hooked on texting themselves and then they'll have no choice but to get off your back.

2. Occasionally, call them just to say "hi." Don't ask for money and don't ask for a later curfew. Casually mention you just wanted to see how they're doing. It gets them every time.

3. Observe all cell etiquette (see The Secrets of Cell Etiquette). Parents love polite teenagers. Simple cell-phone etiquette will win you big points, and you can remind your parents how polite you are when they start getting on your case about how much you text your friends.

4. Lose the attitude. If your parents ask you to turn your phone off at dinner, don't give them trouble. Just do it. The less trouble your phone causes for your parents, the less likely they are to complain about it. Plus, you can always get your messages after mealtime.

5. Don't go over your minutes. EVER. Nothing pisses off parents more than doling out extra cash because your social life is in crisis. If you do go over, play it cool. First and foremost, apologize. Then remind your parents how polite you are when it comes to your cell and promise to keep better track next month. This may keep you from getting in deeper trouble.

The Secrets of Cell Etiquette

1. Keep your ringtone volume at a normal decibel level. Getting woken up by "Girls Just Want to Have Fun" won't make for a happy mom or dad.

2. When you're out with someone, be with them. (If you're talking on your phone, you might as well be somewhere else.) Don't answer calls on a date, and don't text when you're in a movie or at family dinner. If you have to leave your phone on, turn it on vibrate so it doesn't interrupt anyone.

3. Don't be a loud talker. (You've seen the *Seinfeld* reruns.) People around you don't care that your best friend's boyfriend dumped her last night and they don't want to hear about it.

4. When you're dealing with someone, whether it's at the cash register or in line at a concert, don't talk on your phone and do the transaction at the same time. It's just rude.

5. If you borrow someone else's cell to make a call, keep it short so you don't use all their minutes. And be sure they have free long distance before dialing out of state!

6. Don't talk and drive. Some states have laws against teens using cells while behind the wheel, remember?

How to Stay Under Your Minutes

Try to sign up for the same cell-phone company your BFF has. A bunch of companies offer free calls in-network or give you unlimited minutes in the evenings and on weekends. Being able to call your best friend for free will save you lots of minutes and save you (and your parents) from those killer overage charges!

Time Warp

The first prototype cellular system wasn't invented until 1977, and cell phones weren't commercially available until the 1980s—and even then they weren't common. How old were your parents then?

Here's another good reason you NEED a cell: Your cell phone can actually help you study for the SAT. The Princeton Review has a program that allows you to prep for the SAT test on your cell. You can program your phone to ask you test questions, and your parents can even get the results e-mailed to them. Might not sound like the best option, but if you can keep your phone and get into a good college, why not? Parents won't try to stop their kid from studying, and you might score even higher when you take the exam. Just a whisper of the word "scholarship" will have your parents drooling. Who knows? They might even spring for a new phone. (Google "The Princeton Review" for more info on cell-phone SAT prep.)

Just the Facts

Studies show that teens who talk on their cell phones a lot are less likely to take up smoking. More than 50 percent of teenagers have cell phones. Don't you deserve a little respect? You are helping the economy, after all.

Parents Talk Back

Going over your minutes might not be the only reason your parents don't like cell phones. One mom has other worries: "Cell phones are creating a generation of kids that don't know how to talk. They get together, break up, and carry on entire relationships without ever speaking to one another. However, I love being able to get ahold of them without calling 20 friends to track them down. (That is, assuming they answer my call and not pretend that their phone was turned off. This seems to happen around curfew time.)" —Julie, 50

When Mom or Dad Threatens to Take Away Your Cell

• Remind them how handy it is when they want to check in.

• Pester them about safety. Every parent wants their kid to be safe. What if you were in an emergency situation and didn't have a way to call home? When's the last time you saw an actual pay phone? And even if you found one, would you know how to work it?

• Offer to try a pay-as-you-go phone. Your parents won't have to worry about getting caught with a huge bill of overage charges and usage fees, and you'll still have a phone. It's a win-win.

• If all else fails, beg. Promise never again to go over your minutes and to be the best teenager in the history of the entire world. And if you make this promise, keep it! (Sometimes crying a little helps, but

don't throw a huge pity party. You want them to feel bad for you, not think you're a spoiled brat.)

If you can't convince your parents that your cell phone is bettering your life, both healthwise and educationally, try the good old Kill 'Em With Kindness approach. Your parents really want to know what's going on in your life. So let them in a little. Sure they're totally clueless, but it won't kill you. And it might help your cause. If nothing else, tell your parents you want to go grab a bite to eat and catch up on life. After you pick their jaws up off the floor, make a show of turning off your cell phone before you head into the restaurant. (They'll be putty in your hands.) The whole thing will

only take an hour or so, but your life will be smooth sailing for at least a few weeks. Plus, it's free food, and that's definitely worth a couple of missed calls.

Breaking News: Your Parents Aren't Just Old, They're Deaf Too!

For those sticky situations when you don't want your parents to hear your phone ring (e.g., you're supposed to be doing homework), you can download a ringtone that most parents and adults can't hear. It's actually a really annoying high-frequency beep that will probably give you a headache, but if it will keep your mom from hearing your phone ring at midnight, it's worth it.

Parental Training Tip

Show your parents how to download some cool ringtones for their phones. You won't have them constantly nagging you about your "obnoxious" ring anymore because they'll have one too!

Time Warp

When your parents were teenagers, they used typewriters and kept a bottle of Wite-Out at their desks. Can you imagine life with no backspace, no spell-check, no Google? ARGHHHHH!

IM'ing and the Internet

When it comes to your parents' technology issues, cell phones are only the beginning. Chances are, they hate instant messaging and freak when you spend time on the Internet. But again, it's because they're ancient. Even though your parents think they're up on the latest, they think "lol" is short for lollipop and have no clue that "PoS" means "parent over shoulder." And those are old school! You might as well be speaking another language.

But you can convince your parents that sitting in front of the computer for hours at a time is a good thing. It just takes a little maneuvering and some statistical data. What parent doesn't like to hear the facts?

Internet Defense #1.

Every time you log on, you're learning how to multitask. Can your mom or dad really e-mail, instant message, chat, search, blog, and download MP3s at the same time? That takes some serious skill. Just imagine how well you'll do in college!

Internet Defense #2.

Most teens are considered the Chief Technology Officer of their houses. How many times have they asked you a question about the Internet? CTOs at big companies earn big bucks, and as the CTO of your house, you definitely deserve some respect (and more time online).

Internet Defense #3.

The Internet has some serious educational value. Next time your parents give you crap about staring at the screen for hours at a time, tell them that according to a national survey by AOL, more than 50 percent of teenagers use online resources to get help with their homework, and that number gets bigger every day.

Internet Defense #4.

Just because you're on the Internet doesn't mean it defines you. There are just as many adults online as there are teenagers, if not more. Plus, do your parents want to be defined by the trends of their generation: polyester, macramè, and blue eye shadow? Didn't think so.

But what if your parents' biggest complaint isn't how much time you're spending online but rather that you don't have any computer manners? Here's where some basic Internet etiquette comes in.

• If you use the family computer, get your own log-on. That way, when you set a new background or change the cursor, you aren't screwing up any of your parents' settings. It's not like you want to look at your mom's daisy wallpaper 24/7 anyway.

• If your parents ask what you're doing online, tell them the truth. Don't say you're doing homework if you're not. (Hint: Throw in a few questions about your English homework when you're IM'ing your best friend. You'll be doing some homework and, who knows, you might actually do better on the test.)

• If your mom or dad needs the computer for an emergency, be flexible. But ask them to be flexible with you, too. They might not think it's a crisis when Jen breaks up with her boyfriend, but you do. And that counts.

• Don't leave food or old Coke cans sitting around the computer. This has nothing to do with your parents. It's just nasty.

Cyber-Social Butterflies—Blogging and Online Communities

Just the Facts

Almost 50 percent of teenagers with access to computers have blogs. And only 10 percent of adults do. They don't know what they're missing out on!

Can you imagine writing your deepest, darkest secrets . . . on a piece of paper? That is so pre-Internet. When you have something to say, you just turn on the computer and let it all out on your blog. What you did last weekend, what you want in a boyfriend or girlfriend, what you think about the latest single from your favorite band—anything and everything. And it freaks your parents out. Aside from sharing your secrets with strangers, they're worried that your cyber-social activities will come back to haunt you. Colleges, employers, and even future boyfriends have access to your rantings, so remember to keep it real and reasonable. That might not appease your parents, but at least you won't have to worry about your blog blocking your future.

Have you ever seen that old '80s movie *Back to the Future*? If not, add it to your Netflix queue—it's a classic parent-teenager film. Michael J. Fox goes back in time to 1955, when his parents are teenagers, and everything they're doing is so outdated. Forget hip-hop, skateboards, and computers. His parents are hanging out at drive-ins and listening to "oldies"!

This is totally what the Internet is like for you and your parents. When they were teenagers, they wrote their day-to-day thoughts in journals and diaries and locked them with a little key to keep their parents and nosy siblings from reading everything. They couldn't imagine Web logs, online communities, or social networking sites like Friendster and MySpace—the Internet wasn't even invented yet. No wonder they're freaked!

Why Your Parents Hate Blogs and Online Communities (and What to Do About It)

1. They're worried about Internet predators.

And hey, so are you. You don't want some psycho stalking you any more than they do. So be sure to protect yourself and keep your personal information—like your address, home and cell numbers, school, and even your real name—just that, personal. You can be online, and even have a blog, without revealing all your personal details. (Plus, making up a user name is part of the fun.)

To get your parents to stop stressing, you need to let them know you're being smart about the Internet. (After all, you probably know more about it than they do.) Tell them that you're watching out for yourself by keeping personal details offline. If they're still freaking, show them your profile and maybe even let them see a blog entry or two. Or, if you don't want them having total access to your blog, get one with password protection and let them in occasionally. Hey, it might be good for them to see a different side of you—the thoughtful and creative side. Not only will they be happy to see you expressing yourself, they'll see how responsible you are about being online. And that should get you a little breathing room.

2. They don't want you talking to strangers— or taking candy from them.

Your parents are terrified that whenever you're online, you're meeting up with total strangers. What they don't get is that all your friends are online and you're mostly just chatting with people you already know. Your generation has this new social scene and it's happening on the Internet, not at the malt shop or bowling alley. Just because you're hanging out online and in chat rooms doesn't mean you're being stupid and putting yourself at risk.

Explain to your parents that you wouldn't go to a sketchy neighborhood in the middle of the night, and you won't go into a sketchy chat room either. Ask them to trust you, and then be smart about what sites you visit and who you talk to online so they have reason to. Tell your parents they need to give you a chance; there are good and bad things about the Internet, just like everything else in life. They need to start appreciating the good things. After all, you don't plan on taking candy (or anything else for that matter) from a stranger at the gas station, so why would you do it online?

3. They don't understand why you want other people to read your "diary" entries.

The thing with blogs and chat-room postings is that they're supposed to be interactive. That's the whole point. Your friend from school or from across the country can comment on your latest entry or share a story or joke that fits in with what you're writing about. It's this huge network of people that can back you up or say why they don't agree. You can vent, ramble, show videos, collect links, store pictures, write poetry, and anything else you can think of—all on your own customized Web page, designed however you want. It's a totally new way of expressing yourself.

To get your parents to relate, you have to put blogging in terms they understand: your blog is like a journal that people can read and react to. It just happens to be online and not in a notebook.

You could also suggest that your parents try their own blogs. (Of course, you'll have to help set them up with one.) Tell them it's like therapy, in a good way. Just be careful: Once they see how cool blogs are, they'll be hooked. And then when are you going to get time on the computer to write your own entries?

4. They're worried you'll post something you'll regret.

What happens on the Internet stays on the Internet—forever. Once you post a thought or picture on your blog, it's floating around in cyberspace and can technically be accessed by anyone, anytime. Your parents are used to just shredding personal documents and POOF! they're gone. It scares them that people have been fired from their jobs for blogging about work, kids have been suspended from school for posting threatening things about teachers and other students, and colleges are scouring the Internet for profiles of applicants.

Basically, your mom and dad don't want to get a call from the principal or another parent about something you've put on your blog, and they don't want you to post something that might cause trouble for you in the future. Tell them not to worry. You're not blogging to trash-talk or threaten anyone. Promise you'll be careful about what you write. Follow this rule: If you wouldn't scream it on the street corner, don't put it on your blog.

Remember to be really careful with pictures. They can be just as personal as your name and social security number. You definitely don't want to be the next Paris Hilton. Trust me. It's never a good thing to have any sort of video (or anything else) of you circulating on the Internet. You think you have parent problems now.

5. They think you're pouring your soul into a machine.

And you are, sort of. But it's a machine with people connected to it. More people than you could get on the phone at the same time. Being online instead of talking face-to-face doesn't mean you don't have real friendships. It just means the way friends talk to each other has changed a little. You're actually connected to more people online than you would be at the mall or some after-school club, but to prove to your parents that you aren't becoming an antisocial geek, pick up the phone once in a while and call someone who cares. Just be sure to remind your dad that it was his idea when he starts nagging you about talking on the phone too much.

Chapter ELEVEN

ParentSpeak—Decoding Your Parents' Catchphrases

Sometimes talking to your parents is like being on a study-abroad program. You'll be in the middle of a normal conversation, and then BAM! your parents pull out some random phrase that makes absolutely no sense and expect you to understand the hidden meaning. You and your mom might as well be speaking different languages. If you were really planning to study abroad, you wouldn't get on the plane without a handy little phrase book. So, why would you consider talking to your parents without studying up on ParentSpeak? Now you can translate your dad's catch-phrases and decipher the hidden-meaning behind your mom's famous tone.

Standard ParentSpeak—What Your Parents Really Mean When They're Talking to You

"Because I said so." = This one has multiple meanings.
1. I'm not really sure why I'm making you do this, but I know I should have a reason.
2. I'm the adult here.
3. I'm too tired to argue. (Warning: Don't push too hard after this

one. It usually signals an imminent breaking point, and you definitely don't want to go there with your parents.)

"When I was your age . . ." = Things have changed so much and it's freaking me out.

"You'll thank me later." = I know you're pissed, but I think this is for your own good. I'm just not sure how to make you understand that, so I'm saying this lame line.

"I can't wait until you have a teenager." = I hope your kids make you as crazy as you're making me.

"I don't even know who you are anymore." = I'm scared that I'm losing you. I just want to keep you safe.

"You need to learn from other people's mistakes." = I hate to see you keep screwing up. You know better than that.

"How's school?" = Please just tell me anything about your life. Anything.

"You need to take some responsibility." = Show me you know what it means to act like an adult.

"That's inappropriate." = I'm shocked, or at least I'm trying to act like I am. Chances are, I've probably done exactly what I'm saying is inappropriate.

"You're grounded." = I have no idea how to punish you and the only thing I can think of is locking you up.

"One of these days . . ." = I don't know what I'm going to do, but one of these days I'll think of something.

"Tell me about . . ." = When your parents pull this one out, they're digging for something. This is their way of starting up a conversation without putting you on the defensive.

"Why can't you be more like so-and-so?" = Obviously, this means so-and-so is either totally lame or knows how to impress adults—a good skill to have when it comes time for negotiation.

"What were you thinking?" = Sometimes you are such an idiot, but I can't say that because I'm your parent.

Necking = Old-school lingo for making out

Parking = Making out in your crush's car

Adolescent = What your parents will refer to you as when they want to show they are older and wiser

Tone Deaf: It's All about the Tone

Every teenager knows the real meaning behind ParentSpeak lies within the tone. When your mom says, **"Where did you get that sweater?"** she could be saying:

- What store is that sweater from?
- That sweater looks horrible on you.
- Where did you get the money to buy that sweater?
- Is that your sister's sweater? Did you ask her permission?
- I told you not to share clothes with your friends anymore.

Your dad says, **"Why don't you stay in tonight? We haven't seen you in a while."** It could mean any of these things:

- I miss having you around.
- I don't want you hanging out with that boyfriend of yours.
- I don't trust your friends.
- I'm trying to get you to stay home so we can have a heart-to-heart.

When it comes to figuring out your parents' tone, you have to follow these two steps:

1. Consider the context.

Your mom comments that you haven't had much homework lately. Before you assume she's coming down on you for not studying, think about the "setting" of the conversation. Were you two just chatting about life before she said that? If so, maybe she's just making a simple observation. But if the conversation started because your report card was less-than-impressive, then chances are she does have a deeper meaning.

2. Listen.

Yeah, yeah. You sat there for every word your dad said about your new boyfriend keeping you out past curfew, but did you really hear

him? If you listen to what he's actually saying, you might realize that it's not the curfew he's worried about—it's you. He's not telling you to stop dating the guy. He just wants you to be safe because he loves you. Once you realize your dad is just concerned about the curfew because he loves you, it's hard to be pissed. Listening is everything.

And remember, if you aren't a mind reader then your parents aren't either. If you've really listened to your parents and taken context into account, and you still can't figure out what they're implying, ask. A simple "What's that supposed to mean?" might be your only choice. Just remember to keep the sarcastic tone out of it!

Parents Talk Back

Your parents aren't the only ones whose sayings need decoding. Here are the teen catchphrases that drive your parents crazy:

"In a minute.' When getting off the computer, coming to dinner, getting ready for bed, etc., a minute seems to translate into some undetermined looooong period of time." —Lisa, 48

And she isn't the only parent who feels that way.

"'Yeah, wait a sec' is a common answer for anything I need done. 'Wait a sec' in teenage speak translates to 'Fat chance' in reality." —Elaine, 49

Acknowledgments

I want to thank my amazing parents, Dave and Julie, for inspiring this book. (After all, they really needed some training!) Without them, I never would have realized how clueless most parents are and how much parents and teenagers can learn from one another. Mom and Dad, thanks for being so supportive and having such a good sense of humor. You've been great sports to go along with this. I love you.

My teen queen sister, Jennie, and teenster brother, Connor, deserve their own shout-outs—they gave me perfect advice and spent hours reading chapters, telling me their secrets, and trusting me with their friends. There's no way I could've written this book without their help.

Without my incredible husband, Grant, who supported me through the entire process and offered a totally different teen perspective, I never would've made it past the first chapter. He kept me laughing and on my toes with every page. I love you, Grant. And thanks to his wonderful family, my in-laws: Lucy, Paul, Suzanne, Burton, Kent, and Marilynn.

My sisters Annie and Katie helped me remember all our crazy teen adventures and what troublemakers we were. Their husbands, Erik and Mike, suggested their own brilliant parent-proof strategies and had some hysterical stories of their own. I can't wait until they have teenagers.

Of course, I wouldn't have made it through high school and my own parental training experience without my friends. Kathy went above and beyond the call of friendship—editing my spelling errors, brainstorming new sections, and laughing with me whenever I needed it. And here's a special thanks to Bridget, Chrissy, Jill, Heather, Sean, Brian, and everyone else for sharing their ideas on how to raise my parents—and theirs.

My agent, Djana Pearson Morris, believed in this book from the get-go and was tireless in her work to get it published. It would still be just an idea without her.

This book was truly a collaboration with my editor, Traci Todd. Her thoughtful editing, helpful encouragement, honest advice, and great sense of humor made the entire process fun and productive. Without her, this would be a very different book—and that's not a good thing!

I also want to think Bella Pilar for her fabulous illustrations, Victoria Rock for her wise insight; Mariana Oldenburg for her wonderful design; Cathleen Brady, Chris Boral, and Jessica Levy for their fantastic marketing and publicity efforts; and the rest of the talented team at Chronicle Books.

And finally, thank you to all those teenagers who sent me totally honest input and one-of-a-kind ideas for training every kind of parent. This book is for you!

Index